W9-CCO-808

Also by

MAURICE SAMUEL

Blood Accusation

Little Did I Know

The Second Crucifixion

The Professor and The Fossil

Certain People of the Book

Level Sunlight

The Devil that Failed

The Gentleman and the Jew

Prince of the Ghetto

Web of Lucifer

The World of Sholom Aleichem

These are Borzoi Books, published in New York
by Alfred A. Knopf

Light on Israel

LIGHT
on
ISRAEL

BY

Maurice Samuel

NEW YORK

Alfred · A · Knopf

1968

This is a Borzoi Book

Published by Alfred A. Knopf, Inc.

PUBLISHED MAY 13, 1968
SECOND PRINTING, MAY 1968

 Published in the United States by Alfred A. Knopf, Inc., New York, N.Y., and simultaneously in Canada by Random House of Canada Limited, Toronto. Distributed by Random House, Inc., New York, N.Y. Manufactured in the United States of America.

Library of Congress Catalog Card Number: 68-14882

CONTENTS

MAPS

Note to the Reader

I have tried to enclose within a small compass the essentials of my views and feelings on the State of Israel and the Jewish people as they relate to each other, to world history, and to the contemporaneous world scene. This is a very large subject, but a full and documented statement would not serve my purpose, which is to present the summary of a lifetime of thought and observation.

Side by side with the exposition I have supplied a short factual account of the roots, struggles, and achievements of the Zionist movement, and of the Israeli state, showing by what stages the current situation has been reached. In effect, what I offer is both a primer and a commentary which issues from and outlines a Jewish life-philosophy.

The theme is wide-ranging and must be elucidated from many related points of view. There is a connection between the Christian appropriation of the Jewish Bible, which turned the Jews into usurpers of their own heritage and the Christian-Mohammedan (Jewishly derived) sanctification of Jerusalem which would turn the Jews into usurpers in their own capital. There is a wider connection between these developments and the continuity of anti-Semitism in the Czarist and Soviet regimes. Again, a consideration of modern anti-Semitism leads into the role of world Jewry in the all-human struggle against the debasement of nationalism. I hope that the overall unity of concern will be more readily perceived in a short work.

NOTE TO THE READER

An avowal of partisanship is not a plea for intellectual license. Once the framework of predilection is granted, the reasoning must be honest, the objective facts truthfully reported. It is by these two criteria that I would like the thesis to be judged.

MAURICE SAMUEL

Light on Israel

NOTE ON MAPS

The four maps that appear on the the following pages will be useful in clarifying the narrative part of the text; but in their sequence they constitute by themselves a brief, graphic survey of the vicissitudes of the Jewish state in the making and in realization.

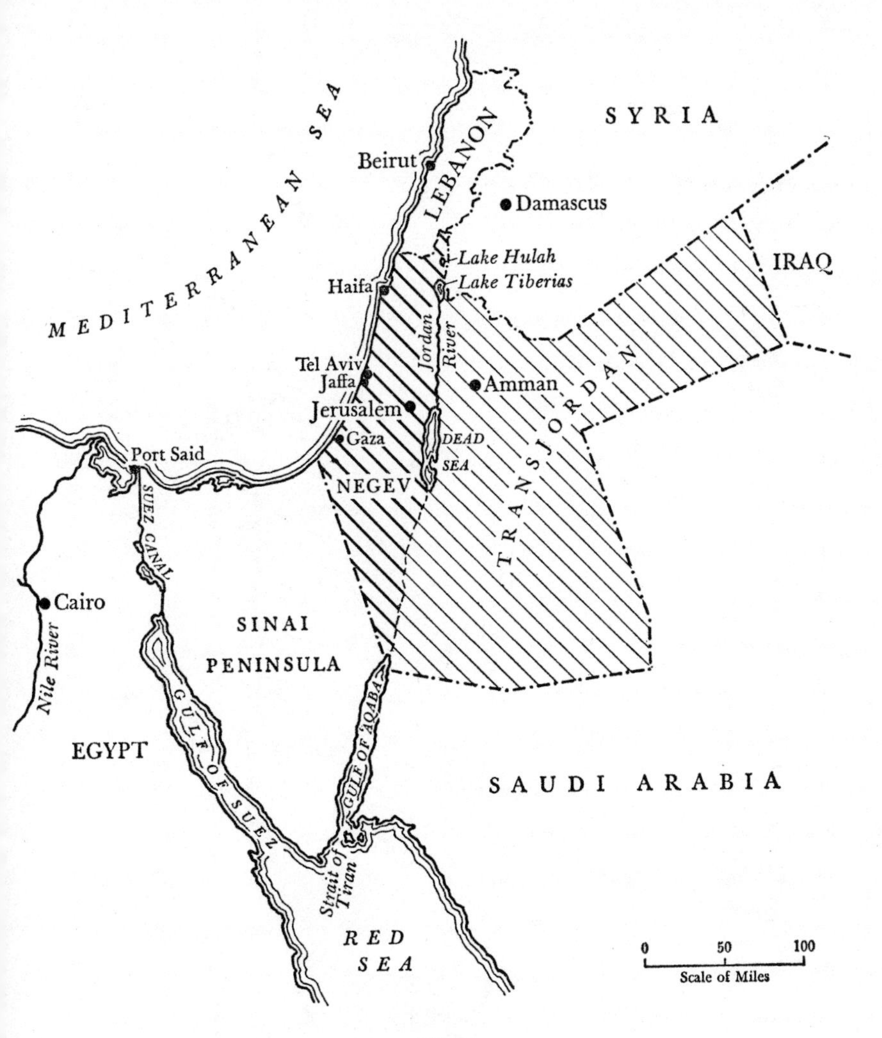

MAP 1

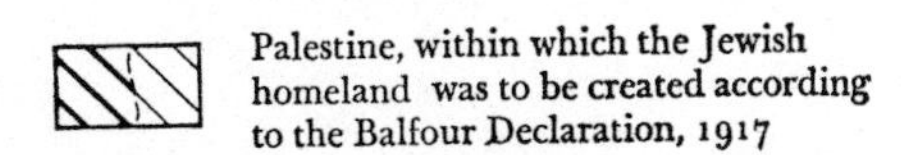

Palestine, within which the Jewish homeland was to be created according to the Balfour Declaration, 1917

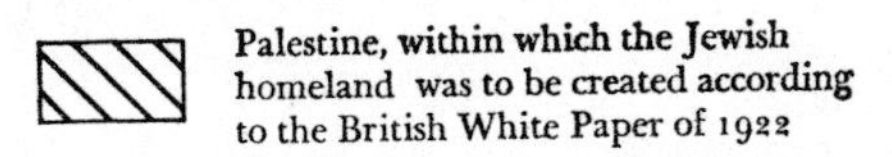

Palestine, within which the Jewish homeland was to be created according to the British White Paper of 1922

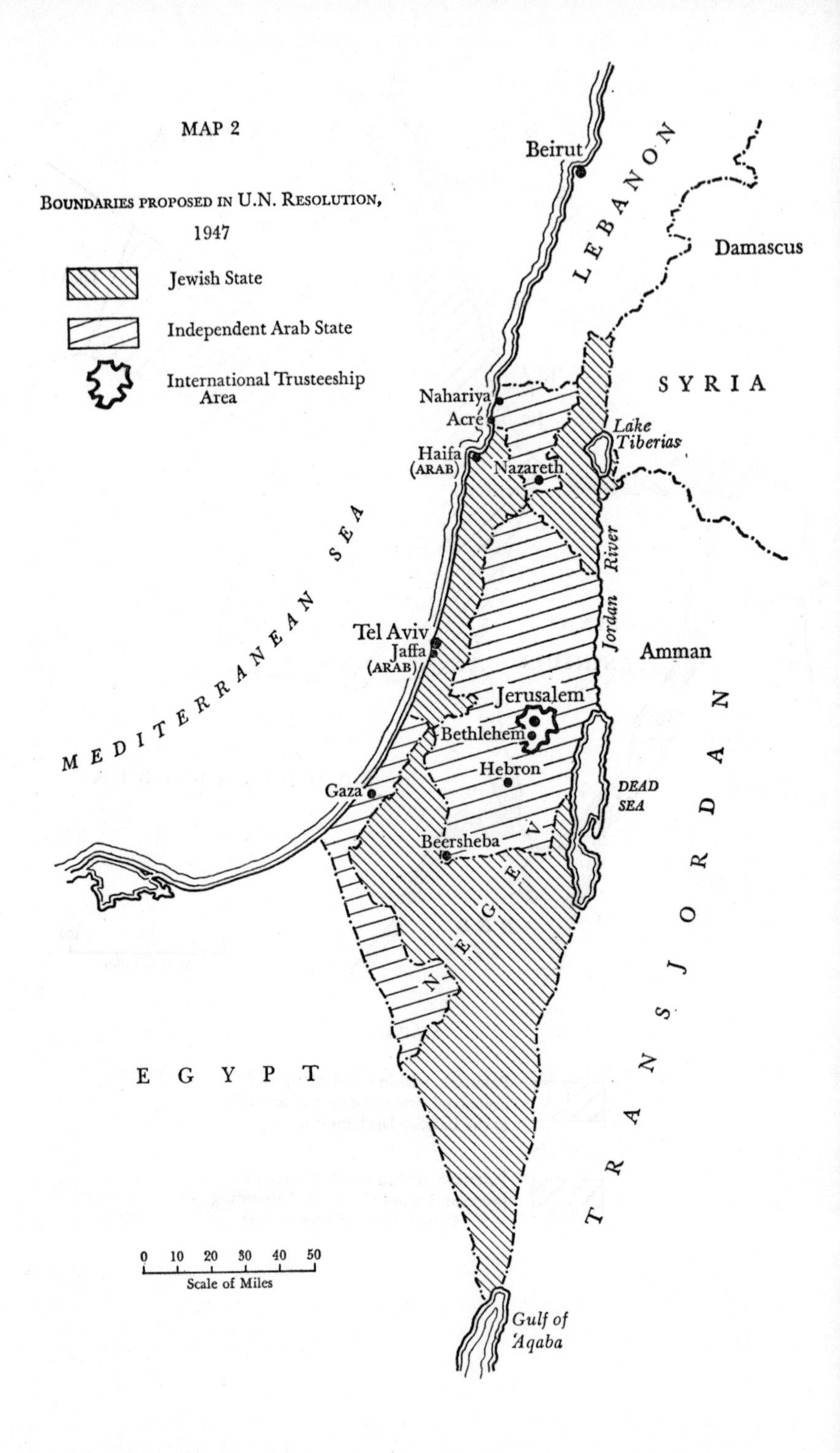
MAP 2
Boundaries proposed in U.N. Resolution, 1947
Jewish State
Independent Arab State
International Trusteeship Area
Beirut
LEBANON
Damascus
SYRIA
Nahariya
Acre
Haifa (ARAB)
Nazareth
Lake Tiberias
Jordan River
MEDITERRANEAN SEA
Tel Aviv
Jaffa (ARAB)
Amman
Jerusalem
Bethlehem
Hebron
DEAD SEA
Gaza
Beersheba
NEGEV
TRANSJORDAN
EGYPT
0 10 20 30 40 50
Scale of Miles
Gulf of 'Aqaba

MAP 3
Israel after War of Independence, 1948
Emirate (later Kingdom) of Jordan
Beirut
LEBANON
Damascus
SYRIA
MEDITERRANEAN SEA
Lake Tiberias
Haifa
Nazareth
Jordan River
Tel Aviv
Jaffa
Amman
Jerusalem
Bethlehem
Ashkelon
DEAD SEA
Gaza
GAZA STRIP (EGYPTIAN)
EMIRATE (later Kingdom) OF JORDAN
NEGEV
EGYPT
0 10 20 30 40 50
Scale of Miles
Elath
Gulf of Aqaba

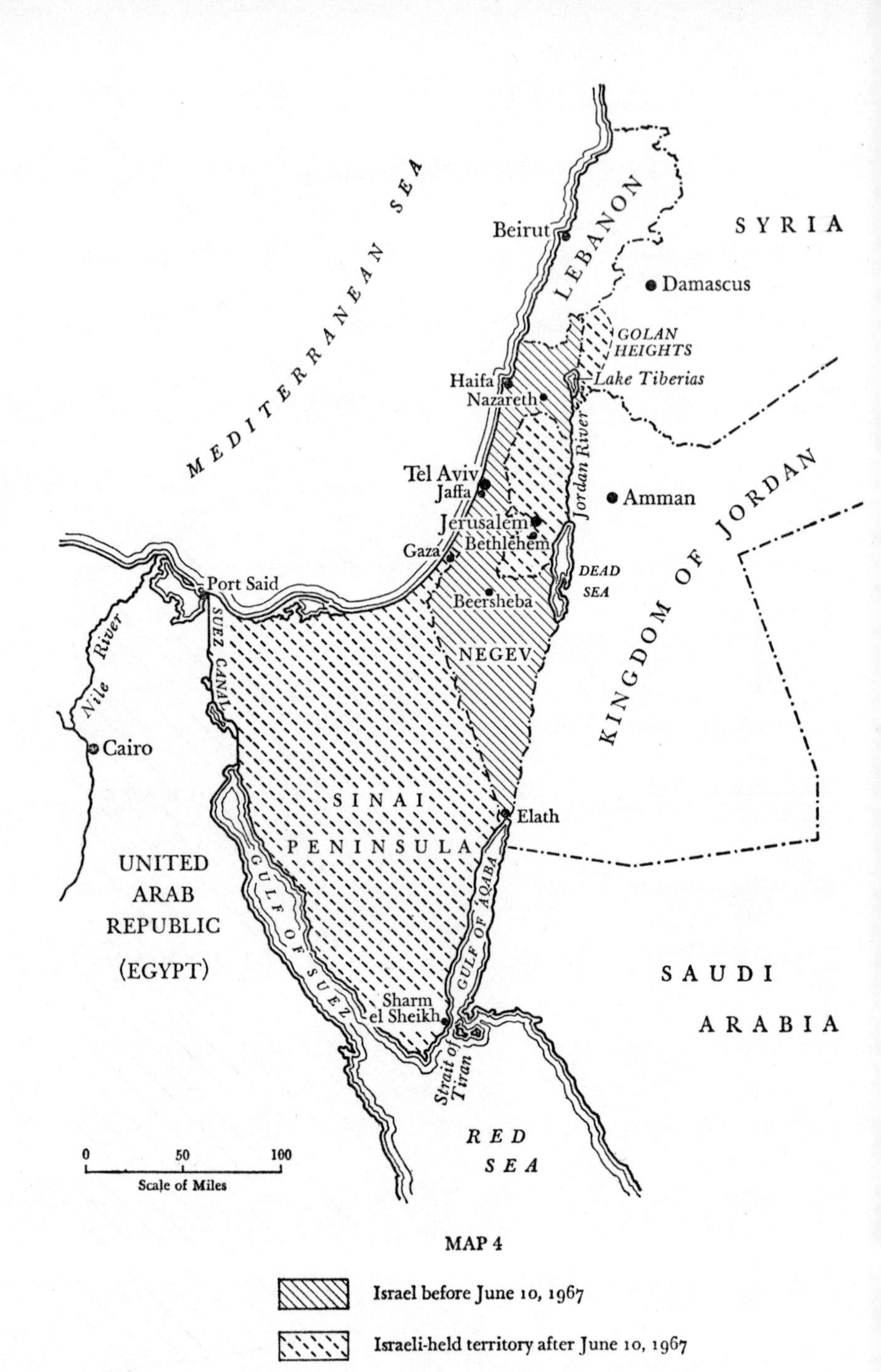

MAP 4

Israel before June 10, 1967

Israeli-held territory after June 10, 1967

1

The Shock of Self-identification

THIS book is written in love and anger, by a Jew who all his adult life has held the belief that the Jewish people still has a creative function in world history, and that an indispensable instrument of the function is the Jewish state or homeland on its ancient site. This belief has grown stronger with the years, and recent events have given it such freshness that a restatement has become a compulsive necessity.

My memory of myself and my surroundings goes back nearly seventy years, and I do not recall as passionate an eruption of Jewish self-identification as that which began toward the latter part of May 1967 and reached its climax in the following month. Nor does anyone I have spoken to or heard of. Nothing like it has been recorded in modern times, and we cannot make comparisons with the remoter past because of the changes that have come over the Jewish people in the last two centuries.

The eruption was not confined to Jews identified with Jewish life through its religious or secular institutions, or to Jews who had an affirmative though undefined relationship to their people. In large areas long regarded as lost beyond recovery to Jewish history, there was a deep shaking up into Jewish self-identification. Thousands of academicians and intellectuals who had "risen above" so special an interest, hundreds of thousands of workers, executives, professionals, businessmen ("ordinary people," as we say) who had drifted from rather than risen above it were suddenly pulled into an anguish of concern for threatened Israel. Aware peripherally of her existence, if at all, and certainly until then indifferent to it, they were moved to horror by the prospect of her destruction, experienced an anguish of relief and triumph when she overcame the threat by her own heroic exertions, and rushed forward, unsolicited, to participate politically and financially in Jewish history.

It was thus in every country where Jews may express themselves freely and from which we can receive uncensored reports. But something also happened in those countries where active Jewish self-recognition is a criminal offense and straightforward information on Jewish life is unobtainable. Direct and indirect evidence affirms that there too Jews were deeply moved by the events in Israel. The warning statements issued in Russia and Poland, provoked by Jewish solicitude for the fate of Israel, are enough to prove that neither voluntary nor enforced assimilation has reached the proportions officially claimed.

Most of the "reawakened," as I shall call them, were not at all aware that they were "participating in Jewish history." Some I have spoken to repudiated the suggestion, or were even offended by it. "It's a purely human thing," they said. "The whole world is stirred by it. The papers are full of it; all other news has been pushed off the front page. Two and a half million standing up to fifty million, seventy-five million, a hundred million, who want to annihilate them." Others said with pride, "Liberals and progressives, and the liberal left in particular, are on Israel's side: in America,

France, England, Germany—everywhere but in the Communist bloc, and even there stifled voices are heard protesting against the official line. Only the stupid confuse this issue with the issue in Vietnam."

All this was true except as it applied to the speakers. The near-unanimity of the non-Jewish emotional and intellectual response to Israel's danger and her escape from it was indeed remarkable; but if it had had the same quality as the Jewish response, the Jewish names in the list of the Israel Emergency Fund would have been washed away. The truth is that for the vast majority of "alienated Jews"—there were of course exceptions—the events of May and June 1967 had special meanings. Perhaps the first of these was related to the obscure psychic discomfort that the Nazi Holocaust had left even among alienated Jews. They had never got over the insinuation that Jewish cowardice accounted for its extent. Six million that went down, as it seemed, without a struggle! Here was the answer. Give Jews their freedom and put weapons in their hands, no more apologies and explanations, also no more Buchenwalds and Bergenbelsens and Auschwitzes. For this vicarious redemption they paid gladly and generously.

Were this the only meaning, there would be little satisfaction in the Jewish response. But there were other meanings, and another kind of Jewish pride. Israel's breathtaking victory focused the world's attention on her nonmilitary achievements, without which her victory would have been impossible. For once the ability to fight was rooted entirely in creditable qualities. For once it could be said that the winner deserved to win, not simply by virtue of the elementary right to live, but because of what he represented.

There were reasons that went deeper and were imperfectly seen. The six-day war awakened ancestral voices rarely heard by alienated Jews. The Israeli victory was a "miracle," and though the word was used in its loose colloquial sense, the pure and awesome original sense was also present. The old, old stories of divine intervention at the last moment, when all seemed lost, recurred to thousands who had but the dimmest knowledge of the Book of their people. This had happened before, long, long ago and in a far-off land—the very land that had just been saved; it had been forgotten, or dismissed as legend unworthy of a modern man's attention. But here it was, before our eyes. And the fact that it was not a miracle made it all the more miraculous.

But for those familiar with their people's heritage there were details of circumstance that seemed almost designed to bring the biblical world to life. Six days the war lasted: for it is written, "Six days shall thou labor and do all thy work . . ." The agonizing consultations and hesitations among the Israeli leaders . . . Is it not written, "And David inquired of the Lord, saying, 'Shall I go and smite these Philistines?' And the Lord said unto David, 'Go and smite the Philistines.' " Most vividly the bloodthirsty raving and ranting of the Arab leaders, contrasting with Israel's restraint, recalled the arrogance of Sennacherib and the dignified silence of King Hezekiah. "Let not Hezekiah beguile you," was the boastful message of Sennacherib to the men of Jerusalem assembled on her walls. "Neither let Hezekiah make you trust in the Lord, saying, 'The Lord will surely deliver us, and this city surely shall not be given into the hand of the King of Assyria.' . . . Hath any of the gods of the nations ever delivered his land out of the hand of the King of Assyria? Where are the gods of Hamath and Arpad? Where are the gods of Sepharvaim, of Hena and Ivvah? Who are they among all the gods of the countries, that have delivered their country out of my hand?' But the people held their peace and answered him not; for the King's commandment was: 'Answer him not.' "

Those and many other passages and pictures swam up

from the Book of Books in minds not entirely estranged from it since childhood. But more powerful than individual hints and intimations was the total evocation, the biblical resurgence into contemporaneity, the startling sensation of *déjà vu.* And the question arose in countless minds: This Israel, this central scene and concern of the Bible, has it been born again after two thousand years in nothing more than a blind and senseless twist of history?

Whether it was a sharpening of religious insight or an onset of superstitious awe, the effect was the same—an awakening of kinship with the past and a sense, even when denied, of a role in Jewish history. Of the alienated who were caught up in the great moment of self-identification some will surely drift away again, with, perhaps, occasional recollection. But many will be permanently changed by the experience. They will realize that their re-entry into Jewish history enhances their worth to themselves and to others, and in time they will come to wonder at the life they once lived. They will find in Israel, as the focus of world Jewry's creative will, their self-justification as Jews, lacking till then. They will know what it is to be Jews by action, not by reaction.

Going deeper, they will also find anchorage in a past of immense richness antedating by far that of other living peoples, and they will marvel at the continuity of purpose as well as of identity. It is written that the story began with Abraham, who made a covenant with God, and in the covenant was pledged to found a people that would serve the world, be a blessing to the families of the earth. It is written that the covenant was renewed to the people, Abraham's descendants, gathered at the foot of Sinai; and it is written, again, that the fulfillment of the pledge was linked forever with the land of Israel. If this is only legend, we are faced with a truth as wonderful as any legend, for we must ask: At what point, and for what reasons, did our remote forefathers take upon themselves so burdensome and uncalled-for a destiny, fastening it upon themselves retroactively in the name of mythical ancestors? Whether its origin be legend or literal truth, the Jews have struggled with that destiny for more than three thousand years. At times they seemed ready to relinquish it, but always, perversely, obstinately, they resumed it, and always the pledge was there, to serve the world. The creation of the State of Israel is one more resumption of the destiny.

It is nearly half a century since I first saw the frail beginnings taking shape in all but desolate Palestine. It was not easy then to hold on to the belief that out of these would emerge a great force renewing the Jewish will throughout the world. But I had teachers whose faith was greater than mine, and they had thrown themselves into the task when the beginnings existed only in their minds. Incapable of doubt, they projected colonies and villages and towns and institutions of learning, and foretold the growing and revitalizing interaction between the homeland that was unborn and the Diaspora that was dying. And I have lived into the fulfillment of their prophecies.

The last of my many sojourns and visits took place soon after the war of June 1967. In the old days I used to come by sea, sometimes by way of Egypt, but latterly it has always been by air, and on this occasion I approached the land in midafternoon, with the sun behind me. And when Tel Aviv came into sight, brilliant along the shore, I caught at my heart in happiness and love. I saw, hidden beyond the horizon and the hills, Jerusalem and Haifa and the colonies of the Emek and of Galilee, the schools, the universities, the orchards, the grain fields—all the abundance of life with which we have filled the land. I was aware also, at that moment, of the Jewry I had left behind me, caught up in a great resurgence of self-realization; I felt that I was a messenger between the Diaspora and the homeland. I wanted to call out to the whole of Israel, "You have done that which has been foretold of you; you have sent through world Jewry an awakening such as it has never known before."

Then for a moment my happiness was interrupted by a flash of horror and anger. "*This* they would have turned into a desolation!" My anger was directed not at the wretched dupes who were sent against Israel, but at those who sent them—those manipulators of men for whom falsehood is the key to the salvation of mankind, and to whom the living are the manure for the doubtful harvest of a future generation. The anger passed, and my mood was again one of love as I descended to the land.

2

The Claim

(I)

TO GET at the substance of the Israel-Arab complex we must go back to fundamentals and beginnings. We must not try to assess the realities only on the basis of recent developments. New facts have obscured old facts that have not lost their validity, and forces that are still operative are being ignored.

Thus the relationship of the Jewish people to Israel, and the existence of Israel itself, are being discussed almost exclusively in terms of the past twenty or thirty years, as though the long past that gave birth to the present were not still at work in it. The claim of the Jewish people to its ancient homeland is made to rest on Hitlerite anti-Semitism, or at most on the neo-Zionism born in the nineteenth century. This restricted view robs the claim of its millennial weightiness, and turns Israel into an *ad hoc* enterprise more or less improvised, without reference to historical realities, to meet a special and unforeseen situation.

But the essentials of the situation are older than Western civilization itself. The Jewish people has never come to terms with the destruction of the Jewish state. Even when so reduced in numbers as to stand on the verge of extinction, it has never seen the Exile as anything other than a provisional condition. Over the millennia it has watched empires emerge and disappear, each heralded as the ultimate in human achievement, and has known itself to be exempt from their common fate. One may say not too fancifully that in its first, or Babylonian, Exile, the Jewish people was given a trial run in the art of survival. The biblical literature of the first Return sank deep into its mind, and throughout the second and much longer Exile, in lands unknown to their forefathers, successive generations of Jews called daily on the God of history to make a second restitution. It is true that during these twenty centuries there was a constant drainage of defection; sometimes in trickles, sometimes in large spates, Jews surrendered, out of weariness or under duress. But a folk remained, and that is what counts. And those who have lived with the folk and shared its ways, who have sat weeping through the Ninth of Ab, the traditional date of both destructions, who remember the weeping of their parents and grandparents at the reading of the Book of Lamentations, know how immediate and burning was the feeling of desolation.

There is no parallel to the phenomenon. Seen from the outside, it is unnatural that for sixty generations a people should nurse its sorrow with undiminished freshness, should rehearse as if they were personal memories the details of a calamity which antedates by centuries the birth of its contemporaries, and proclaim continuously and consistently, "That land is ours! We shall return." Seen and felt from within, the experience was untouched by any sense of the artificial or exotic. But we must bear in mind that interwoven with the mourning there was always a bright strand of rejoicing. Daily at his meals the Jew thanked God for the broad and beautiful land which He had deeded to His people forever. At the appropriate season he celebrated with song and symbol the harvests he was not reaping, and prayed fervently for the rains that would make them more bountiful. He was even careful to specify the kind of rain he wanted: the *yoreh,* the rain of the late fall, and the *malkosh,* the rain of the early spring, suitable for a subtropical climate, though he himself might be living in a temperate or even polar zone, or in a ghetto where he never saw the sun and any kind of rain was an affliction. It could be said of the Jew that he was taking care of the land *in absentia.*

But this last sentence must be modified. There was never a time when there were not Jews in the land called Palestine, and now Israel, representatives of the legitimate owner, whoever might for the moment be in possession. To live in the Holy Land was always one of the highest *mitzvoth*—commandments or good deeds—even though mass reimmigration waited on the appearance of the Messiah. There were even periods of substantial immigration, settlements of pietists and mystics, whose prayers and speculations and conjurations were meant to hasten the advent of the Messiah. The popular notion that with the crushing of the Bar Kokhba revolt in the year 135 Palestine was emptied of its Jews is quite erroneous. The Temple had been destroyed nearly seventy years earlier, now the harrow was drawn through the sacred city and on the ruins a new city was founded, Aelia Capitolina, in honor of Hadrian the conquerer. But there was still a Jewish community in Palestine, scholarship flourished, a measure of recognition was accorded to the remnants of the conquered; the Patriarchate, headed by a succession of great scholars, still sent out legal and religious decisions to Jewry in exile and retained the spiritual leadership until the rise in the fourth century of the Babylonian schools, founded by scholars trained in the schools of Palestine.

Throughout the long darkness of the Middle Ages flashes of light reach us from Jewish communities in Palestine. Toward the close of Byzantine rule, an attempt was made to convert the Jews forcibly to Christianity, and twenty-six thousand of them joined the Persian invader in protest. A century and a half later, under Moslem rule, a brief Messianic fervor seized the Jewish community with the discovery of a sacred manuscript purportedly the work of the great second-century sage Rabbi Simeon ben Yohai. In the tenth century, according to an Arab historian, the Christians and the Jews had the upper hand in Jerusalem, and a Jew, Menasseh ibn Ibrahim al-Kzaz, was governor of Palestine. More than a hundred years later the city was stormed by the Crusaders in 1099; the Jewish community took shelter in the synagogue and perished in the flames when the building was set on fire. But Benjamin of Tudela, the famous twelfth-century traveler, records the existence of Jewish communities in Palestine in his day, and the Jerusalem community was rebuilt by pilgrims from the west. By the middle of the fourteenth century there was a considerable Jewish population in Palestine. In the sixteenth century Safed, with two thousand Jewish inhabitants, was a great center of learning. It was there that Joseph ben Ephraim Karo compiled the *Shulkhan Arukh,* the code of laws, which is still valid for Orthodox Jews throughout the world. The Palestine community was the springboard from which Sabbatai Tzvi, the pseudo-Messiah, was launched on his brief and tragic career in 1666.

A new immigration of Jews began with the nineteenth century, preceding by more than half a century the neo-Zionist movement, and today's strictly orthodox community of Jerusalem is their direct descendant. In the minds of these Jews, as in those of all immigrant groups since the Destruction, there was no thought of instituting the great Return. They were drawn irresistibly to the land by its sacred associations; but whatever their conscious motivation, they were constant reminders, reregistrations of the Jewish claim, appeals against any suggestion of a statute of limitations.

They represented the tenacity of the relationship between the entire Jewish people and the land. No Jewish community anywhere in the world, however dominant it became, ever spoke to exiled Jewry with the tenderness and intimacy of *Eretz Israel,* the Land of Israel. A messenger from one of the four holy cities—Jerusalem, Hebron, Tiberias, Safed—was always received with love and wonder; and I remember out of my childhood the stir that was created in our poverty-stricken North England ghetto when the word went out: "A Jew from Eretz Israel will be at the synagogue this coming Sabbath."

How could it be otherwise when every Jewish child was taught the word Jerusalem almost as soon as it could lisp? The heroes of the Bible were the subject of daily conversation; they were referred to with casualness as well as with reverence; their deeds were discussed like those of contemporaries, except that contemporaries were never quite so real, for contemporaries might die, or might do unexpected things, but those heroes would always be with us, and would never let us down.

The landscape of Palestine, or Eretz Israel, dominated the earliest visual imagination of Jewish children. Long before they had taken their local topographical bearings they were familiar with Mount Moriah, where Abraham had been ready to sacrifice young Isaac, and where Jerusalem rose later; with Carmel, where Elijah discomfitted the prophets of Baal; with the valley of Sharon, whose roses were like King Solomon's Sulamite; with Hebron, where the three patriarchs were buried; and with the tomb by Ephrath near Bethlehem whence the fourth matriarch, the universally beloved Rachel, issued nightly to weep for her children because they were not. They had wandered through the desert and stood at the foot of Sinai, they had rested in the oasis of Kadesh-barnea, they had heard the tremendous valedictory of Moses on the plain of Moab, and dry-footed they had crossed the Jordan with Joshua to begin the conquest.

And still the power of these vision-realities cannot be grasped without their ever-present cosmic obbligato. These are the archetypal experiences of man, whose search for God gives us the only acceptable meaning to the creation of the universe. The poignant and indestructible longing of the Jews for the Holy Land was far more than an extraordinary vitality of nostalgia, more also than an equally indestructible hope of escape from physical vagabondage, insecurity, and humiliation. It was the will to continue the search first incorporated in the land, in its heroes and topography. Through those men, among those scenes, the attempt had begun to create a moral standard for all mankind, and the history of that attempt is the essential history of the Jewish people. All its other achievements, however impressive they may be, are incidental. And wherever else Jews might settle, even in large numbers, and perhaps permanently, the land was an indispensable instrument for the continuation of the attempt.

For the land was the basic expression of social law. Man did not own it; he was a lessee under God. Its produce was not exclusively his own; part of it belonged, as of right, not as an act of charity, to the widow, the orphan, and the stranger. This was the law, the only one of its kind in the ancient world, and in an extended sense a model for the Western world. It was also the law that no lessee might be permanently dispossessed—however he had lost the tenure, through misfortune or neglect, it was restored to him in the Jubilee year. None of these provisions were touched with the repellent aspects of "philanthropy." They were commandments.

The study of the commandments, side by side with their practical application, was in itself the supreme commandment. The Jew did not accept the principle of moral intuitiveness, and purity of heart was not regarded as the sufficient guide to right conduct. He was bidden to meditate on the law day and night, for "the ways of the heart are dark, who shall know it?" and without the trained and well-informed mind goodness is easily perverted. If the Bible assures us that it is enough for man "to do justly and love mercy and walk humbly with his God," it also warns us repeatedly that without intellectual discipline man is incomplete and therefore morally defective. In no other people has the study of the Law been made a religious obligation for the ordinary citizen, and a cultivated mind a prerequisite for perfect worship. In one biblical passage we are admonished to be a kingdom of priests, but the overall directives point rather to a republic of saintly, subtle, and learned jurists.

"Israel, the Torah, and God are one" is the great summation offered by the Zohar, the mystical book of the Middle Ages, which also affirms that as long as there is no Jewish homeland, the Divine Essence, or *Shekhinah,* is itself in exile. These are extraordinary statements for a people that first proclaimed and has most obstinately maintained the oneness and ubiquity of God. They must be read as hyperbolic expressions of frustration that say in effect, "As long as we have not rebuilt our homeland we are not ourselves."

(II)

A SYMPATHETIC OUTSIDER with a liberal turn of mind, surveying this picture, may be moved to say, "This is indeed a phenomenon without a parallel, and in its way touching. But in this world of ours, which is what it is, what does it all lead to? You cannot have peoples refusing to accept the verdict of history and clamoring for two thousand years, which is practically forever, against a *fait accompli.* Fifty or a hundred or two hundred years is as long as any people may reasonably demand a restoration such as you claim. It's different with the Greeks, for example, who have remained on their own soil and constitute a majority there. But when a people has been pushed out into distant places, or has been completely overrun and submerged, the thing is unmanageable. One might as well talk of returning America to the Redskins, India to its Dravidians, Egypt to its Coptic (i.e., Gyptios—Aegyptios—Egyptian) minority, England to the Welsh—the list is endless. If the Jews have chosen not to forget, or are somehow incapable of forgetting, it is their misfortune, not the world's responsibility. We are ready to acknowledge what has not always been acknowledged, and even today is not acknowledged everywhere, and that is the right of the Jews to maintain their religious and cultural identity wherever they may live, and we shall protest vigorously against any infringement of this right. But as to your right to build a homeland in Palestine, that is an entirely different matter. As it happens, you've done it somehow, and we can't deny that it is in itself a rather fine thing. To be sure, when you first set out to do it we liberals thought it quite ridiculous as well as reactionary—not to mention impossible. For that matter, we didn't see any point in this business of Jewish survival, and some of us still don't. But we, unlike you, are willing to accept a *fait accompli,* and we must admit that Israel has been a godsend to the Jewish refugees. We also admit that you are owed some kind of restitution after that horrible Hitler episode. We didn't come out of it well—I mean we, the democracies; and that inclines us all the more to support your Jewish state—within reasonable limits, naturally. Why aren't you content to talk of Israel in realistic terms as the product of a contemporaneous situation? Why do you brood over the irrelevancies of two thousand years, and stake out a claim on the basis of your folk fantasies, which are none of our business?"

It all sounds quite decent, if a trifle sheepish, but consciously or not, it is dishonest through and through. "Your folk fantasies, which are none of our business . . ." I do not say that if Christendom had behaved differently toward the Jews they would have vanished, or at least overcome their haunting sense of loss. But when the Western nations took over the Jewish Bible—which is, among other things, the Jewish national record—as an essential and by far the more voluminous part of their sacred writings, they undertook to keep alive, as an article of faith, the association of the Jews with the Holy Land. And how insistent they have been about it! The Jews simply have not been permitted to forget. Not only was it dinned into their ears century after century after century that by their refusal to acknowledge the Messiahship and Divine Sonship of Jesus they had forfeited their homeland, not to mention their right to remain Jews; they were forcibly reminded that they had even forfeited the right to their own interpretation of their Bible! From the time of Justin Martyr, the first patristic theologian, who was a contemporary of the final destruction under Hadrian, down to this day, the taunting has gone on, emphasized periodically by expropriations, expulsions, proscriptions, pogroms, and baptism under duress. If the Jews protested that they did not want to listen, they were sometimes herded into churches and made to listen, for their souls' good; if they said, "We'd rather not talk about it," they were told, "By God and His Son, you will," and with infinite reluctance they entered into compulsory debates in which their opponents were the judges.

"O fair hill of Zion!" "O excellency of Carmel!" "Balm of Gilead." "Sweet vale of Sharon!" The Christians could not get over the beauties and benedictions of the land. To be sure, they were speaking symbolically most of the time, but with a fervor that could not but mislead a non-Christian. If the Jews had not themselves been familiar—much more familiar than the Christians—with these and a hundred other haunting phrases, they would still have been goaded by such wistful repetitions into torments of regret. "Your land was destroyed and you have been made homeless because you crucified Jesus" was the everlasting refrain, begun by Justin Martyr. "See what would still have been yours if you had not rejected Him."

Not less galling, if less effective, was the attempt to expel the Jews from possession of the Bible itself. "It is not your Bible, because you do not understand it. Degenerate sons of glorious fathers, you have no portion in it. For you perversely refuse to see that the whole purpose of your, or rather your fathers' Bible, now ours, was to prepare the coming of the Christ. It was of Him that your prophets and singers spoke and sang. It is because you are wilfully blind in all your generations that you will not recognize the obvious allusions to Him in Isaiah 4, 7, 11, 28, 31; in Ezekiel 36, 37; in Micah 4, 5, 7; in Zechariah 6, 9, 14; in Canticles everywhere—and these are only a few instances."

If the visions of the prophets and the consolations of the Psalmist spoke as intimately and comfortingly to the Jews as to the Christians, that was by a pure delusion, and a kind of intellectual misappropriation, a fraud committed on the sacred text by the descendants, according to the flesh, of those who had composed it, and an affront to the heirs according to the spirit, for whom it had been composed.

For these reasons it is improper for Christians to dismiss the claim of the Jewish people to its ancient homeland as a private fantasy for which *they* have no responsibility. Nor can they speak of it as a thing of the remote past, a historical curiosity. It is a historical thing in the most living sense, an effective element in the thinking of the Western world, and its presence can be denied only by an act of evasion.

I dwell on this point because if it cannot be established, the State of Israel is trivialized into an accident. I dwell on the continuity of the claim from ancient times because it is a permanent feature of the history of *Christendom,* and later, in a more relevant context, I shall try to show how effective the element is, and how skillful the evasion. But here I will only examine some part of the process that has thus conditioned the mind of Christendom and what the consequences have been.

When Saul of Tarsus opened up the division between Judaism and Christianity, he could not have foreseen what it would do to the Jewish people, for he was willing to let the Jews retain all that was Jewish—circumcision, the Sabbath, the festivals, the entire national ritual and culture—and all he asked of them, as of the rest of mankind, was to accept Jesus as Savior, Soter, Messiah, and Son of God. For some centuries there existed a Jewish sect, a branch of the Ebionites, which did in fact conform to this view. It hovered between the total disapproval of the Jews and the uneasy and diminishing tolerance of the Church. But by the time of the prepatristic fathers, it was already being denounced as a dangerous "Judaizing" element, and in the second century Justin declared that the Sabbath and circumcision had been imposed by God on the Jews as a mark of His displeasure, so that they might be singled out for the execration of mankind. Two centuries later the sect was denounced by the Church as heretical, and it disappeared.

The compromise was natural to Saul, who sought to be all things to all men. When he declared that there was no longer Jew or Greek or barbarian, he certainly did not mean that the nations would lose their identities, their languages and literatures. Certainly he did not demand that the Jews give up their language and literature and cult. Certainly he did not demand that they cease to be a people. This was what the Church demanded, seeing in the peoplehood of the Jews the matrix of their blasphemous religion. And when the Jewish state was destroyed the Church rejoiced, nor has it to this day become reconciled to its reconstitution.

As for the people itself, the Church, too, entered into a compromise, but one very different from Saul's. The Jewish people was accursed; not only had it been guilty of the Crucifixion, but it was the obstacle, if only by its very existence, to the total conversion and salvation of mankind. Yet though the Church was bitterly hostile to the Jews, it did not want them to disappear entirely, not even by voluntary mass conversion. For a double role was assigned to the Jew: he was at once a welcome and corroborating witness and a hateful and horrible example. He vouched for the authenticity of the Old Testament, the underpinning of the New, and he demonstrated the dire consequences of rejecting the Christ. He was the brother of the Christ and the embodiment of Satan. As a Jew he did not deserve to live, but as a Jew he had to stay alive for the apotheosis of the Second Coming. Buffeted between these opposing attitudes, the Jew survived, building himself local habitations the duration of which depended on his usefulness to the laity and the mood of the Church.

It remained for the twentieth century to produce a segment of Christendom which found the ambiguities of the double policy intolerable, and in a characteristic fit of thoroughness adopted a program of total annihilation with no escape through conversion. Germany may have had special reasons, not only of character but of circumstance, for reaching this frightful decision; but we cannot absolve the Church, as it acted throughout the ages, from a great share in the responsibility. Sooner or later the millennial cat-and-mouse game was bound to get on someone's nerves, and the cry would go up, "For God's sake, let's get rid of this Jewish problem once and for all. No more paltering with concessions and half measures. *Die entgültige Lösung,* the Final Solution! Wipe them out—all of them, men and women and children, and let the world at last be *Judenrein.*"

The word genocide was coined to express the uniqueness of Germany's crime against the Jews, and much has been written concerning the beastliness with which it was carried out. But genocide is not a new thing. Peoples have been destroyed before so that their territories might be occupied, and the Jews were not the only ones toward whom the Germans harbored genocidal intentions. Revolting cruelties, too, are a familiar feature of human history. The peculiarity of Germany's superbly organized extermination of the Jews was its idealism, its practical pointlessness. A complicated and exacting industry of death was created and maintained at a high cost to the war effort. Large numbers of men—planners, executives, workers—vast quantities of building material and rolling stock, not to speak of much inventive ingenuity, were placed at the service of the enterprise when they could have been used to great advantage elsewhere. To round up and butcher six million hogs calls for considerable investment of funds, labor, and equipment; to do that with six million human beings is far more complex and costly. We simply cannot understand it unless we realize that the German leaders and the tens of thousands who worked with such a will at the unnatural business were convinced that the destruction of the Jews served a high principle, which for some transcended the welfare of the *Vaterland* itself. Certainly there was a sadistic thrill that spurred the diligence of the executions; but, dimly or clearly, the killers could hear the applause of their country and of humanity, and this, with the consciousness, dim or clear, of God's or history's approval, added the last touch of ecstasy to their sadism.

If I repeat that this unique aberration owed as much to the cumulative effect of Christian ambivalence toward the Jew as it did to a special set of circumstances, it is for the purpose of assigning responsibility rather than guilt. The Holocaust came—and this has a profound significance—at a time when the Jews had demonstrated on the soil of their forefathers the vitalistic quality of their attachment to it. During one of the breathing spells of partial permissiveness, they had done to the land what no one else had succeeded in doing since their expulsion: they had brought it to life and re-endowed it with contemporaneous significance for the world. They had proved that what they had not wanted to forget, and what the world had insisted on their remembering, had been waiting for its hour, and that the hour had struck. But even as the hour of redemption struck, the hatred of the ages gathered itself together to deny it fulfillment in the total extinction of Jewish life.

The Jewish people had stopped supplicating. Defying the tradition which bade it wait for a Messiah, it had taken its destiny into its own hands. It had resolved to become its own Messiah, announcing to the world that it could no longer tolerate the ambivalent status imposed upon it—the very resolution reached by Germany, but with a diametrically opposed objective.

A German victory in World War II might not have meant the literal, total obliteration of the Jewish people; but it would have meant something hardly less appalling. With Nazi collaborationist governments in Europe, the work of the death camps would have gone forward to completion. Here and there handfuls of Jews would have lived out underground lives of terror and starvation. The Jewish homeland in the making would have been uprooted. What would have happened in an isolated and embattled America is harder to imagine, but most certainly the forward democratic surge of the previous years would have been violently reversed. Darkness in Europe, twilight in America, and everywhere the theme resounding: "It was the Jews who brought this calamity upon the world," resounding so insistently that the Jews in their hiding places would begin to repeat it, adding, "Better if we had never been born."

The Nazi attempt on the life of Jewry was not the justification of the Jewish homeland. That can be the view only of those for whom history begins with themselves. The farther-sighted know that this *Attentat* was only the latest—though the most shocking—assertion of a thesis established by the Church many centuries ago and maintained into our own times.

3

The Occupants

WHEN the Arabs adopted Mohammedanism they did not, like the Christians, take over the Jewish Bible *in toto*; nor did it become for them a peripherally sacred book. They did, however, take over many of the principal and some of the minor heroes of both Testaments, to such an extent that without them the Koran, which is of about the same length as the New Testament, would be practically devoid of human characters and would hang in a void of doctrinal exposition. Abraham and Moses appear with great frequency throughout, and Noah is accorded an importance, or at least a degree of attention, which quite overtops his role in the Bible. The story of Joseph is told with much circumstantiality, and in his case even more than the others, many details are added from Jewish extrabiblical tradition. There are fewer references to Jesus, and his Divine Sonship is rejected as blasphemy. David slays Goliath, just as in the Bible; Pharaoh is frustrated, so is his minister Haman, transferred to his reign in Egypt from that of Ahasuerus in Persia; the great literary prophets are nowhere quoted, and of the others only Elijah and Elisha come in for mention. But the prophets are spoken of in general terms, and they, like the other protagonists of both Testaments, are praised for the purity of the messages they brought to mankind—messages that the Jews and Christians alike have perverted in their own lives, and that would have been lost if Mahomet (to use the more familiar form of Muhammad) had not appeared with the true and final restatement.

But what Mahomet got—and this chiefly from the Old Testament—besides the flesh and blood embodiment of his dissertation, was his blazing monotheism and that immediacy of rapport with God which, as in Jewish doctrine, makes inconceivable the notion of an intermediary, much less, then, a "Son of God." Mahomet proclaims himself a human being, born as all human beings are born, subject to death like all human beings, destined like all true believers for resurrection on the Judgment Day. He is a participant in the common life, he marries and begets; like Abraham he has concubines as well as the "true wife"; like Abraham he has business dealings with his fellow men. What lifts him above all human beings is the unique and final revelation or series of revelations brought to him by the archangel Gabriel, and written down or dictated by him (the tradition is not clear on this point) over the years.

Theologically, Mohammedanism is much nearer than Christianity to the spirit of the Jewish Bible. A religion proclaiming an Emanation or Son of God clothed in human form for the salvation of mankind does not need the Jewish Bible for its corroboration; and to the Jew it seems that the insistence on this corroboration does violence to the biblical text. In other words, doctrinal, if not ethical Christianity could have been born without the Jewish Bible; in fact, it existed in other forms outside the Jewish world. But Mohammedanism without the Jewish Bible is inconceivable. Still speaking doctrinally, Christianity's debt to Judaism is fortuitous, that of Mohammedanism is organic and total.

This may explain why ancient Palestine did not become the "Holy Land" for Moslems as it did for Christians. The identity of Mohammedanism would have been lost. Jerusalem is only one of its three sacred cities, ranking after Mecca and perhaps Medina. It is called in Arabic *el Kuds,* "the holy," the word being akin to the Hebrew *qadosh.* It was from Mount Moriah in Jerusalem, the site of Isaac's sacrifice and Solomon's temple, that Mahomet ascended to heaven on his steed *el Burak* to confer with God. The rest of Palestine is no more sacred to Moslems than Italy is to Christianity in spite of the sanctity of Rome, where Peter and Paul suffered martyrdom by fire and Ignatius was thrown to the lions. And here again the special debt of Mohammedanism to Judaism stands out. Mecca and Medina are sacred to the Moslems because in those cities Mahomet lived and labored. But Jerusalem had been sacred to the Jews for fifteen centuries before Mahomet was born. It could not be left out, and so it was appropriated by the device of a single visit.

The Koran lumps Jews and Christians together under the name of "the people of the Book," that is, the Bible, but makes a clear distinction in the matter of blood relationship. Jews and Arabs were kinsmen. They were both descended from Abraham, through his sons Isaac and Ishmael. Their languages were as close to each other as, say, French and Italian. They had been in contact for thousands of years —Arabia and the Arabs are mentioned seventeen times in the Jewish Bible. No such ethnic bonds existed between Arabs and Christians, except insofar as Christianity had spread among a small number of Arabs. To the Arabs "Christian" meant the outside world, Rome (actually it was Byzantium, later Constantinople, "Rome on the Bosphorus") which first represented the Western world to the Moslems. The Jews were "our own people," and their unresponsiveness to his message must have produced in Mahomet a baffled incomprehension, perhaps sharper than that produced in the early Christians by Jewish unresponsiveness to the message of the Christ.

In Medina, where Mahomet established himself after his flight from Mecca (the Hegira, in A.D. 622, the first year of the Mohammedan calendar), there were many Jews. They should have been his natural disciples, much more so than his pagan fellow Arabs. They had not been infected by what in his eyes was the disabling superstition of a Son of God. What was he, who claimed to be only a mortal man, saying that offended their faith? Nothing that he could see, but they saw an impiety that horrified them. At one stroke he had wiped away the vast literature and tradition of Mishnah, Talmud, and Midrash, a whole civilization which had resisted Egyptian and Assyrian, Greek and Roman. He was seeking to dispossess them of a heritage of learning and of ethical speculation that, outside of the Bible, had been developed during twenty generations in the schools of Palestine and Babylonia. To be sure, he respected the Bible and its heroes, but he demanded that his version of it replace the original, which was to sink into the obscurity of an outside text.

For the second time, then, a religion rising on Jewish foundations invited or rather commanded the Jews to vacate their place in history, and finding them recalcitrant denounced them for contumacy, blindness, and blasphemy. And like Christianity, Mohammedanism, a continuing force to this day, has made of its indebtedness an occasion for hostility.

Something must be said here about the difference between "Mohammedan" or "Moslem" and "Arab." When the Arabs burst out of their peninsula and within a century created an empire stretching from northern Spain to the confines of China—its area exceeded that of the Roman Empire at its greatest extent—they brought under their rule an immense variety of peoples, Iberian, Berber, Negro, Coptic, Jewish, Iranian, Indian. In the West the religion was predominantly Christian; in the East it was divided between Zoroastrianism and Hinduism. Though Mohammedanism spread almost as rapidly as territorial occupation, the majority of the Jews and some of the Christians held out: the other religions have practically disappeared in the lands held for any time by "Arab" rulers. But the ethnic strains were little affected. The original Arabs were not numerous enough and did not stay long enough to diffuse their racial characteristics—not always homogeneous in any case—through the conquered peoples. We speak today of the "Arabs" of Algeria, Morocco, Libya, Tunisia, Egypt, Syria, Iraq, Saudi Arabia, and I shall continue to use the term, but ethnically it is as meaningless as "Americans." "Moslems" is of course a much wider term, for it includes Persians, Pakistanis, Indonesians, and others; but if the Moslems of the first group of countries all wish to be designated as "Arabs," that is their right, as long as we remember that it is now a political and linguistic, and not an ethnic, designation.

Palestine, at that time held by Christian Constantinople, and itself Christian but for the Jewish minority, was among the earliest of the Arab conquests (A.D. 634–40). North Africa, from Egypt to the Straits of Gibraltar, was predominantly Christian, with pockets of ancient paganisms. Spain was wholly Christian. At one moment it looked as if the Arab tide was everywhere irresistible. Had it not been turned back at Tours in 732, European history would have taken a very different course, and Gibbon would not have been able to observe (with such obvious relish) that "the interpretation of the Koran would now be taught in the schools of Oxford, and her pulpits might demonstrate to a circumcised people the sanctity and the truth of the revelation of Mahomet."

Actually the Arab thrust had spent itself in France, just as the Mongol thrust had spent itself, on the very same territory, three hundred years earlier. There was, however, an immense difference between these two threats to the development of a native European civilization. The irruption of the Huns left behind (in a later and more limited episode) an isolated memento in the gifted Hungarian people, which was absorbed into Europe while retaining its own language. The Arabs (the reader must bear in mind the quotation marks) learning from and surpassing the peoples they conquered, created together with them a brilliant civilization that has woven itself permanently into the fabric of the Western world. No one challenges the statement that if the Arab world had not kept alive, reinterpreted, and developed the wisdom of the ancient world while Europe was struggling out of the Dark Ages, the emergence of the modern world would have been long delayed and it might have lacked some of its most valuable elements.

This rapid excursus into Arab history is necessary in the approach to contemporary Arab problems. The awakening of Arab self-consciousness, miscalled "nationalism" (but again I shall be compelled to use an inaccurate term) by a false analogy with European history, is not like the awakening of primitive African peoples. It is stimulated and exacerbated by the memory of a magnificent past. It would serve no purpose here to go burrowing into details and to ask each group of "Arabs" what share *its* ancestors had in that vanished glory. It suffices that there was indeed a great civilization carried by the Arab language, which all the Arab groups speak. But superb in conquest, the Arabs are dispirited in subjugation. They could transmit their religion (though not their language) to the conquering Turk, but under his rapacious and increasingly corrupt rule they lapsed into apathy and shiftlessness. For a little more than four centuries they were the masters in Palestine and the rest of Asia Minor. From the end of the eleventh century on they lost position after position until by the beginning of the twentieth century most of them had scracely more control over their own destinies than the Negro tribes of Africa.

The Arab record in respect of its Jewish minorities compares favorably with the Christian, which is not saying very much, and it is no consolation to add that the Christian minorities fared no better. Arab or Moslem masses were never interpenetrated by a demonological horror of the Jew as the accursed slayer of the Son of God. The story of the Jewess accused of trying to poison Mahomet in his later years is incidental in the Moslem tradition. The Jew was despised and discriminated against as an infidel. Nevertheless there were great episodes of Arab-Jewish symbiosis, notably in the early centuries. In Spain Jews held high positions at the court and in society; Jewish scholars worked with Arab scholars to the enhancement of their common civilization.

But the situation may, within limits, be compared with that of the Jews of Germany at the beginning of the twentieth century. The success of Jewish writers, artists, merchants, and professionals was not inconsistent with the spread of anti-Semitism, manifesting itself in the social world, in the aristocracy, and the army. But it would be an outrageous injustice to make too much of the parallel. On the other hand, the rejection of the Jew, or of Judaism, by Moslem civilization was deep-rooted. As the fortunes of the Islamic world declined, outright and consistent persecution eclipsed the large areas of tolerance. There was no particular season of the year, like Easter among the Christians, when religious teachers whipped up hatred against the Jews, and there were no spectacular massacres of the Jews, like those of the Crusades, of Khmelnitski in the seventeenth century, Petlyura in the twentieth—and of course nothing like the transcendental wickedness of Hitlerism. There was only a relentless denial of human rights, restrictions in the economic field, mulcting by special taxes (also applicable to Christians), humiliations, enforced conversions, and of course sporadic pogroms. One naturally did not hear among Arabs the ever-recurrent cry, "Jews, go back to your own country," since the Arabs ruled it or were in occupancy. But when Arabs protest that they are being forced, through the acceptance of the State of Israel, to pay for the sins of Christian Europe, they ignore a heavy account of their own. They too, even when they were looking down on the Jew as an inferior, and embodying their contempt in laws and acts, consistently kept alive in the Jew his bonds with the homeland he had lost.

They did not, as I have pointed out, make Palestine itself the idealized cradle of their faith. They did not study the geography of Palestine, as the Christians did, and make knowledge of it a piety. What they did, what they still do, insofar as the Koran is one of their unifiers, has been hardly less effective in keeping alive the Jewish feeling of displacement, exile, and loss. "Why," the Jew could ask, "must you keep reminding us of Abraham and Isaac and Jacob and Joseph and David and Solomon, and of our onetime happiness? You tell us, like the Christians, albeit in other terms, that by our behavior we have betrayed our forefathers and do not deserve to claim them. Thereby you only make them more precious in our eyes and strengthen our resolution to maintain the bond and to honor our covenant with them, according to which the land from which we have been driven still remains ours."

The Jews have been severely chided for calling themselves the Chosen People and thinking of themselves as a unicum. The rebuke comes with poor grace from the Christian and Moslem worlds. It is Christian doctrine that they were indeed chosen, and that in a cosmic sense, to produce the Savior of all humanity; and both Moslems and Christians make of them the peculiar people, small in number, negligible in power, without which neither of them could have acquired their religions. It is not sufficient for the New Testament to imbed Jesus in Jewish life; it uses an extraordinary argument to associate him with the richest of the Jewish traditions, tracing the descent of the father who did *not* beget him to King David of blessed memory. It is not sufficient for the Koran to announce that Mahomet found everlasting truth; it must also maintain that the Jews found it before him, if not in as clear a form, and it must bring forth in array all the figures that Jews revere.

One would have thought that the most elementary sense of gratitude would have dictated an act of restitution to the Christian and Moslem worlds, especially when it was so tiny a corner that the Jews longed for; and if not gratitude, then simple justice, after so long a history of harassment and taunting. But when restitution began, gratitude had nothing to do with it, and though a feeling of justice was not absent from the Christian world, the Moslem world, after some hesitation, raised a loud cry of *injustice.* "It is we who are being made to pay, and we don't want to pay for history. We want a fresh start." But sometimes—alas, not always—history has to be paid for. America is paying for the crimes she committed against the Negroes, as England paid for her crimes against Ireland. But let us not think here of history as record, tucked away in books. Wherever Jews are disadvantaged because they are Jewish—that is, wish to identify themselves as Jews, whether religiously or culturally or ethnically or in any other fashion—wherever the Jew finds the struggle for life harder because he is a Jew, wherever he must be better than his non-Jewish opposite to achieve the same recognition, history is today and not simply in books. Christian and Moslem, Westerner and Arab will answer, "Restitution and justice do not call for the reconstitution of the Jewish state, but for a cleansing away of all manifestations of anti-Semitism." This familiar answer, on the surface so complete, raises fundamental problems that I shall treat in detail later; here I shall only enumerate them. A cleansing away of anti-Semitism so thorough as to foreclose the possibility of reinfection is a far-off prospect. But the creation of a Jewish homeland is infinitely more than an answer to anti-Semitism; and the paradox of it is that if there were no anti-Semitism there would be no opposition to the creation of a Jewish homeland, at least ideologically. More than that, the nonexistence of a Jewish homeland is itself a cause of anti-Semitism, for it is an abnormality, reflecting on the status of the Jewish people and therefore on the status of the individual Jew who elects to remain Jewish. It is further a confirmation of the ancient superstition that the Jewish people forfeited the right to a homeland by an act of deicide.

But what a pity it is that we speak of "paying for history" when we rectify its wrongs. It is as though a man begrudges the money he spends on curing himself of a sickness. All the resentment would disappear if we could see the effort as a voluntary contribution toward our self-improvement.

4

The Beginning of the Snarl

Zionism is as old as the Jewish Exile; neo-Zionism, the notion of the Return as a non-Messianic, practical mass enterprise, was born in the nineteenth century; political Zionism, which is simply neo-Zionism with a political apparatus, was founded at the close of the nineteenth century by Theodor Herzl (1860–1904).

Herzl did not at first understand Zionism otherwise than politically and sociologically. It was for him a great plan to solve the Jewish problem by lifting the Jews out of their hostile environment and resettling them in a territory of their own, not necessarily Palestine. A Westerner, brought up in Vienna and wholly steeped in Western culture, only superficially acquainted with the folk tradition, he was a stranger to the peculiar *Heimweh*, the incurable nostalgia for the Holy Land, which invested Zionism among the masses of Eastern Europe. When, in 1896, he wrote his remarkable pamphlet, *Der Judenstaat* (*The Jewish State*), he knew nothing about the powerful neo-Zionist sentiment agitating the Jews of Russia, Poland, Galicia, and Romania, nothing about the literature it had produced or about the men who were preaching the Return in the cities and ghettos and *shtetlach* of the Pale. Zionism was not for him, as it was for them, a comprehensive double program for the re-creation of the Jewish homeland and the revitalization of the Jewish people everywhere. He learned with a shock of the Jewish thinker Ahad Ha-Am (1856–1927), who envisaged the rebuilt homeland—which could only be in Palestine—as a center of spiritual renewal for all Jewry; and it broke his heart, literally, when Russian Jewry, in the midst of a wave of pogroms, turned its back on Great Britain's (tentative) offer of a territory in Uganda, even though he presented it as a temporary refuge from the Czar and the Cossacks.

Political Zionism began with a search for a patron or protector. Herzl thought first of Germany, and wooed Wilhelm II. Failing there, he turned to England, which offered him Uganda. (Marvelous are the blindnesses of creative genius: Germany, which was to produce Hitlerism a generation later; Uganda, next door to the Mau Mau country.) He died in the prime of his manhood, worn out by his exertions to organize Zionism and to obtain the charter of a homeland from the then ruler of Palestine, the last sultan of Turkey, Abdul-Hamid II—Abdul the Damned. The second great leader, Chaim Weizmann (1874–1952), lived long enough to become the first president of the State of Israel. In vivid contrast to Herzl, with whom he maintained a running battle over the nature, aims, and methods of the Zionist movement, he was of the folk and the tradition, an admirer and disciple of Ahad Ha-Am. From the beginning —remarkably enough, from his early boyhood, as a letter of his written at the age of eleven attests—he believed in England as the instrument of Jewish liberation, and despite many disappointments he stood by this choice almost to the end.

Folk Zionism was wholly democratic, for among other things it was the revolt of the Jewish masses against the wealthy, self-appointed leaders who, well connected with the non-Jewish world, undertook to keep their people obedient to the ruling powers. Political Zionism, conducting as it were the foreign policy, was tinged with imperialism at its outset. Herzl would have lent the support of the movement to the German *Drang nach Osten*; and Weizmann and his circle urged upon England the usefulness of a client Jewish state in Palestine, guarding the Suez Canal and the line to India.

It was not from inclination but from life-and-death necessity that the Zionist movement went through that phase. Without a patron it could not take the first step. There were no great countries that were not imperialistic, and all liberation movements begin with the search for an interested ally, without too much squeamishness over his character (e.g., the early American alliance with France). Still, there was a difference between the two choices: Germany was imperialism on the rise, and her triumph would have thrown back for a long time the universal liberation movement; England's was an imperialism in decline, increasingly tolerant, tired, and approaching abdication. It did not take long for the contradiction between the liberationist spirit of Zionism and the imperialistic purposes of England to be revealed. A confused and complicated relationship set in between the two partners with disparate objectives, and before Weizmann was succeeded by Ben-Gurion—the third in the triad of Israel's founders—the partnership had turned into an enmity.

England's rejected offer of Uganda in 1903 was political Zionism's first victory; it marked the official recognition by a great power of the Jewish right to a homeland. Her Balfour Declaration of November 2, 1917, marked the recognition of the indissoluble tie between the Jewish people and Palestine. Issued with America's concurrence in the midst of World War I, it read:

> His Majesty's Government view with favour the establishment in Palestine of a national home for the Jewish people, and will use their best endeavours to facilitate the achievement of this object, it being clearly understood that nothing shall be done which may prejudice the civil and religious rights of the existing non-Jewish communities in Palestine, or the rights and political status enjoyed by Jews in any other country.

The *quid pro quo* consisted of two parts: the aligning of Jewish sympathy everywhere on the side of the Allies, with an eye particularly on America's three million Jews and on Russia's seven million, recently liberated by the Russian Revolution, and the acquisition of a client state next door to the Suez Canal. This practical aspect of the transaction makes it easy to stamp the Balfour Declaration as devoid of any moral content; but here it happened, as it sometimes does, that selfishness coincided with a disinterested principle. The Balfour Declaration corresponded to a widespread sentiment in the Christian world in favor of the Return, and was in effect the first step toward the righting of an immemorial historic wrong.

A sharp demurrer may be entered here. It is the Arab claim that the Balfour Declaration was the first step in the infliction of a new historic wrong. Its phrasing is ambiguous or even self-contradictory. "Nothing shall be done which may prejudice the civil and religious rights of the existing non-Jewish communities in Palestine." Was it not the civil right of these communities to call Palestine their own and separate country, in which they, as the overwhelming majority—some six hundred thousand versus some seventy thousand Jews—were to set up their own government? Had they not the right to set up a Palestinian nationality, and did not the Balfour Declaration propose to deprive them of that right?

I draw attention to the phrase "set up a Palestinian nationality," for a Palestinian nationality did not exist. Palestine was not the locus of a nationalist sentiment. Professor Philip K. Hitti, probably the most widely accepted authority on Arab history and Arab affairs today, opens his *Syria: A Short History* thus:

> Syria, in its geographical sense, occupies a unique place in the annals of the world. Especially because of the inclusion of Palestine and Phoenicia within its ancient boundaries, it had made a more significant contribution to the moral and spiritual progress of mankind than any other comparable land. . . . As the cradle of Judaism and the birthplace of Christianity it originated two of the great monotheistic religions and prompted the rise and development of the third and last . . . Islam. . . . Closely associated with its religious contribution was the ethical message southern Syria—Palestine—conveyed. Its people were the first to insist that man is created in the image of God and that each man is the brother of every other man under God's fatherhood.

The extinction of the Jewish people in this strange passage, and the appropriation of Moses, Isaiah, Jesus, man in the image of God, etc., to the credit of the Syrians is all very well—who would not like to claim them on the slightest pretext?—but it disarmingly, if unintentionally, makes the point that if Palestine ever had an identity it was because of what the Jews did there. And if the Jews were, after all, nothing more nor less than southern Syrians, their right to reoccupancy is strikingly reconfirmed.

Still the question will be urged: "Did not the Arabs of

Palestine or southern Syria, a majority of seven or eight to one in 1917, have the right to declare themselves a distinct nationality and refuse to have their territory turned into a Jewish homeland?" It is true that a community does not become a nationality, does not acquire the emotions and specific needs of nationality, by a declaration; nevertheless, a community may decide to turn itself into a nationality. Should not such a decision be respected?

I am pushing the Arab argument to its extreme. Not only was there no Palestinian nationalism, there was not even an inclination to create it. But if there had somehow been any such inclination (and its existence would already imply an embryonic nationalism), there is a decisive difference between intention and actuality. In the actuality of a nationalism a corporate spiritual identity already exists; it is entitled to recognition; it must be treated with solicitude. Infringement of this identity is an invasion of the personality of the individual. A man who feels himself spiritually and culturally and psychologically rooted in the fact of a certain nationality must not be compelled to relinquish it. The deliberate destruction of the conditions that nurture his nationalism is a great wrong.

But is it also wrong to disturb the conditions under which a community, if left alone, *might* develop a nationalism? Let me emphasize that I am speaking of *Palestinian* and not of *Arab* nationalism, of the Palestinian Arab's right to develop an as yet nonexistent *Palestinian* nationalism, and not of his right to retain his *Arab* nationalism there, which has never been challenged. To put it otherwise, was it the right of the communities of Palestine, overwhelmingly Arab, nationalistically conscious or not, to be left alone, to do with the country whatever they liked?

If the question is so phrased, the answer must be: "Yes, unless another claim existed." And if that claim, the Jewish claim, which I have tried to establish, is disallowed, the Balfour Declaration was an unjustified act of violence committed upon the seven hundred thousand Arabs inhabiting Palestine in 1917.

Later developments may alter the perspective. The situation of the Jews of Germany after Hitler's advent to power reduced the question to elemental terms. With the rest of the world mostly closed to them, with despoilment and destruction facing them where they were, the German Jews —and later the Jews still unable to escape from territories occupied by the Germans—had to choose between Palestine and death, and they would not choose death. And after them, the hundreds of thousands who survived the death camps, only to find the world still closed to them, had to choose between reconstructing their lives in lands that had become their charnel houses and reconstructing them in a welcoming and helpful environment, and they chose the latter. The picture in the 1940's was totally different from that of 1917, and a reassessment had to be made of the relative rights of Jews and Arabs in respect of Palestine. The Arabs refused to make it, but it could be said by the Western world, including Russia, that the homeland which had its political beginning in the Balfour Declaration had justified itself.

For the Zionists the moral perspective was not altered. Their claims referred to a larger historical perspective and were concerned with more than the refugee problem. They had always seen their relationship to the Arabs in affirmative and creative terms, and at the time of the Balfour Declaration there had been Arabs who shared their views.

(II)

IN MARCH 1919, Dr. Weizmann, the leader of the World Zionist movement, and the Emir Feisal, the leader of the

Arab peoples liberated by the Allies, were both in Paris, at the heads of their respective delegations to the Peace Conference.

On March 3, Feisal addressed the following letter to Professor (later Supreme Court Justice) Felix Frankfurter, an American member of the Zionist delegation:

> I want to take this opportunity of my first contact with American Zionists, to tell you what I have often been able to say to Dr. Weizmann in Arabia and Europe.
>
> We feel that the Arabs and Jews are cousins in race, suffering similar oppression at the hands of powers stronger than themselves, and by a happy coincidence have been able to take the first step forward toward the attainment of their national ideals together.
>
> We Arabs, especially the educated among us, look with the deepest sympathy on the Zionist movement. Our deputation here in Paris is fully acquainted with the proposals submitted by the Zionist Organization to the Peace Conference, and we regard them as moderate and proper. We will do our best, in so far as we are concerned, to help them through; we will wish the Jews a most hearty welcome home.
>
> With the chiefs of your movement, especially Dr. Weizmann, we have had, and continue to have, the closest relations. *He has been a great helper of our cause,* and I hope the Arabs may soon be in a position to make the Jews some return for their kindness. *We are working together for a revived and reformed Near East,* and our two movements complete each other. The Jewish Movement is national and not imperialistic. Our movement is national and not imperialistic; and there is room in Syria for us both. Indeed, I think that neither can be a real success without the other.
>
> People less informed and less responsible than

> our leaders, ignoring the need for cooperation between the Arabs and the Zionists, have been trying to exploit the local differences that must naturally arise in Palestine in the early stages of our movement. Some of them have, I am afraid, misrepresented your aims to the Arab peasantry, and our aims to the Jewish peasantry, with the result that interested parties have been able to make capital of what they call our differences.
>
> I wish to give you my firm conviction that these differences are not questions of principle, but on matters of detail, such as must inevitably occur in every contact with neighboring peoples, and as are easily dissipated by mutual goodwill. Indeed, nearly all of them will disappear with fuller knowledge.
>
> I look forward, and my people with me look forward, to a future in which we will help you and you will help us, so that the countries in which we are mutually interested may take their place in the community of civilized peoples of the world. Yours sincerely,
>
> Feisal.

This letter (to which I have added the italics) does not stand alone. "The proposals submitted by the Zionist Organization to the Peace Conference," which the Arab deputation regarded as "moderate and proper," were also spelled out in an agreement entered into by Feisal and Weizmann two months earlier. Paragraphs three and four read:

> In the establishment of the Constitution and Administration of Palestine, all such measures shall be adopted as will afford the guarantees for carrying into effect the British Government's [Balfour] Declaration of November 2, 1917.
>
> All necessary measures shall be taken to encourage and stimulate immigration of Jews into Palestine *on a large scale* [italics added] and as quickly as

possible to settle Jewish immigrants upon the land through closer settlement and intensive cultivation. In taking such measures the Arab peasant and tenant farmers shall be protected in their rights, and shall be assisted in forwarding their economic development.

The italicized words should clarify what was in the minds of the Zionist and Arab leaders; not, as some have argued, a token admission of Jews, but a solid occupation. This is also evident from the Feisal letter, which contemplated the advantages of cooperation between the Jewish and Arab national movements.

During the course of the war, and before the signing of the agreement and the letter, several conferences had taken place between Feisal and Weizmann, the first of them near Amman (now the capital of the Hashemite Kingdom of Jordan, ruled by King Hussein, the great-nephew of Feisal). Feisal was the commander in chief of the Arab forces assisting the allies in ejecting the Turk from Arab countries. T. E. Lawrence ("Lawrence of Arabia"), the fiery Arab partisan, was the intermediary at the first conference, and continued to serve both sides—he was an equally fiery Zionist partisan—at the Peace Conference. In his autobiography, *Trial and Error,* Weizmann justly points to the negotiations and agreement as an answer "to the critics who have accused us of beginning our work in Palestine without ever consulting the wishes or welfare of the Arab world." The accusation could be truthfully leveled at Herzl; it cannot be leveled at Weizmann. It is almost certain that if the Arab leadership had not been eager to draw a Jewish homeland into the Arab world for the mutual benefit of Jew and Arab, if it had opposed the Balfour Declaration at the Peace Conference, the Zionist movement would have collapsed, to await another occasion. The anti-Zionist elements in England would have got the upper hand then, instead of some years later; for the war was won, and the practical reasons for a pro-Zionist policy no longer had the same force. The Jewish claim to a homeland in Palestine would still have been valid, but it could not have been successfully pressed. There had to exist a recognized coincidence of interest between the Jews and the Arabs, and it existed.

Shortly after Feisal reached his agreement with the Zionists, he added the following condition: "If the Arabs are established as I have asked in my manifesto, I will carry out what I have written in this agreement. If changes are made, I cannot be responsible for failure to carry out this agreement."

He was stating the obvious. What he had asked in his manifesto to the Allied Powers via the British secretary of state was the establishment of a free Syria. Like Professor Hitti he understood under the term Syria the territory from the Taurus to Sinai, including Palestine and what is now called Jordan, but what was then named Transjordan, that is, the part of Palestine lying east of the Jordan River. Within this large territory there was room for populational maneuver. Palestinian Arabs could be relocated by purchase and compensation, involving no change of country. The Jewish homeland could then emerge within the framework of a Jewish-Arab federation.

Unless this is what the Zionist and Arab leaders had in mind, the agreement has no meaning. As Weizmann was to put it shortly afterwards, Zionism was striving for a Jewish homeland that was to be as Jewish as England was English. This was not to say there would be no Arabs in the Jewish homeland or no Jews in other parts of Greater Syria. England, too, has her minorities. In the frustrated dream of the Zionist and Arab leaders, the entire Middle East, equitably apportioned, was to afford room for the peaceful and cooperative development of the Jewish and Arab nationalisms, with Palestine as the area allocated for the Jewish national home.

The area of Palestine on both sides of the Jordan was 44,000 square miles. Much of it was desert, but a great part of that was, as the Jews have proved in the Negev, reclaimable. The possibilities were enormous, but possibilities are seen only by those who have the will to use them, and what the Jews have done in Israel could have been done in the rest of Palestine. Had Israel been permitted to concentrate on Transjordan—and on the Middle East generally—the skills it has scattered through Nigeria, Ghana, Mali, Liberia, Ethiopia, and a dozen other emerging Afro-Asian states, had its social forms penetrated to its Arab neighbors, had its market been open to them, as theirs to her, had the insane arms race been aborted, the Middle East would have been today a radiating center of prosperity and democracy.

And how eager the Zionists were to play that role! With what fervor we used to speak, long ago—it is like another age—of the "bridge" we would build between East and West, and of the rebirth of the ancient center of civilization. How naïve it was, and how valid it still is as the only way out of the dreadful snarl.

It had the naïveté of all great visions that must travel to realization by unforeseen detours. The last and most difficult detour confronts us today; the first was already in the making before the issuance of the Balfour Declaration. The straight road was blocked when Feisal's hopes of a free and united Syria were dashed by the rivalry of the French and British for spheres of influence in the Middle East. Initially an attempt was made to harmonize this rivalry with the genuine interests of the Arab peoples. The now forgotten Sykes-Picot Agreement between France and England—negotiated but never carried out in its original spirit—anticipated a mandatory system very different from the one which was ultimately installed. It proposed the beneficent and transitional tutelage of a divided Syria—the term is used here in its proper all-inclusive sense—with France administering what are now called Syria and Lebanon, and Palestine on both sides of the Jordan assigned to England. The arrangement need not have been inconsistent with the Balfour Declaration; but the two men who negotiated it, Sir Mark Sykes for England, and Georges Picot for France, did not foresee the practical consequences of the division. The rivalry between France and England in the Middle East became so bitter (we might compare it with the episode in World War II, when England was fighting in North Africa and Syria was held by the Vichy French) that the interests of the Arabs were pushed into the background, and the Balfour Declaration began to turn sour for the British.

The Weizmann-Feisal grand plan was never given a chance. When in 1920 Feisal tried to assert his claim as king of an independent Greater Syria, he was thrown out of Damascus by the French, and he wound up, with more good fortune than he might have expected, as king of Iraq, with no say in the affairs of Syria or Palestine. He learned to regret his brief and bright vision of an Arab-Jewish union and to forget the help he had received from the Zionists at a difficult time.

The second road block on the path of Zionist realization, far more formidable than the first, was created in June 1922, strangely enough, when the strongly pro-Zionist Winston Churchill was colonial secretary, and a Jew, Sir Herbert (later Lord) Samuel, was high commissioner to Palestine. Abdullah, Feisal's older brother, having invaded Transjordan with a tiny army, was confirmed as emir of that territory by the British, who had just set his brother on the throne of Iraq. The effect was calamitous for Zionism and Transjordan. The new emirate was an artificial and by itself a nonviable state, not so much because it lacked possibilities but because, withdrawn from the area of Zionist operation, it was doomed to stagnation. The Jewish homeland, which had been offered 44,000 square miles within which to find room for itself and the Arabs, now had to make do with 10,000. A great many of the difficulties and sufferings that have attended the birth of Israel are the result of that unstatesmanlike act of 1922.*

The reader will notice that I have used "Jewish homeland" and "Jewish state" interchangeably. Much has been written about the difference. It has been pointed out that the Balfour Declaration speaks of a Jewish homeland, not of a Jewish state, and the Zionists have been accused of duplicity in the representations of their intentions. But it is difficult to see how there can be a Jewish homeland without Jewish self-rule, and a Jewish homeland with self-rule is a Jewish state. There were undoubtedly some Zionists who thought "homeland" a less aggressive word than "state," but they pulled the wool over nobody's eyes. Actually, "homeland" ("*Heimstätte*" in the original Zionist platform) had a particular appeal to the homeless Jewish people, and it still remains a popular designation for the Jewish state.

* See map, page 3.

5

The Snarl Thickens

NEITHER the Jews nor the Arabs were ready for the Weizmann-Feisal plan. The Jewish longing for the Return was a genuine impulse; so was the surge of Arab "nationalism." Both were handicapped, each in its own way, by historic conditions and internal divisions. Both came unexpectedly into the blinding light of opportunity; both blundered and stumbled. The handicaps were further weighted by developments beyond the control of both.

Neo-Zionism took hold first among the poor and the religious, and at the center of the awakening were the millions of East European Jews. Among the religious I include the secularists who had been brought up in the tradition and had been conditioned by it, even though they were no longer observant Jews. But large numbers of the poor turned to the anti-Zionist revolutionary movements, and many of the pious repudiated a secular folk-Messianism. The rich, with an exception here and there, were as shocked by the Zionists as by the revolutionaries, and where wealth went hand in hand with piety the shock was painful and vocal in the extreme.

At the time when neo-Zionism arose, as in our time, and as at all other times, large numbers of Jews—it is impossible to be statistical here—were abandoning their Jewish identity. To those who would not or could not follow their example, the action was a betrayal: of the God of Abraham, Isaac, and Jacob in the eyes of the religious; of the folk, in the eyes of the secular. However narrow this judgment may seem, it remains a fact that with every defection the position of the loyal Jews becomes more precarious. In the nineteenth century neo-Zionism was the particular reaction of the time and the circumstances to the threat of mass defection. The reborn Jewish homeland was to be the physical rescue of those who elected to go there, the spiritual rescue of all.

Those who were bent on escape—and many were escaping without making a principle of it—regarded Jewish loyalty as an anachronism, and worse. In the form of Zionism it was a perversity, and they reciprocated the contempt and resentment of the Zionists. For just as the latter saw Zionism as a re-Judaizing movement that would improve the status and inner condition of the Jew, so the assimilationists saw in it an assault on their chances for assimilation. They denounced it as offensive to the ideal of universalism, a return to the ghetto, to medievalism and obscurantism. It also compromised their patriotism, which was somehow part of their universalism. It tainted Jews with the suspicion of dual allegiance, and was therefore a weapon in the hands of anti-Semites. They put their trust in "Progress," which would soon make the Jews at home everywhere, and fifty years ago they hailed the Russian Revolution as the collapse of the last citadel of anti-Semitism.

This group has slowly lost its influence and since May–June 1967 has almost disappeared; but its survivors still come out, armed with intellectual flintlocks and fowling pieces, to do battle with the idea of the Jewish state. In the early days of Zionism, however, it was strong enough to discourage the weaker-willed. But even those Jewish masses that were unshaken in their faithfulness to the tradition of the Return did not respond at once to the Zionist call. They were like a patient long bedfast trying to recover the use of his limbs; and a man in that plight is not helped if his first steps are discouraged and derided by his relatives. Moreover, they had doubts of their own. Could it really be done by *them?* Might not this hope of self-redemption dissolve into a fata morgana? Had not these twenty centuries atrophied the faculties of hand, brain, and heart that are the hallmarks of an independent people?

The Balfour Declaration was a great lift to the hopes of Zionists, but no mass rally of action followed it. The Jewish people was less disposed than any other to put its trust in princes and rulers. Did England really mean to give Palestine to the Jews? And if it did, would not someone else take it away? But perhaps the severest blow to Zionist self-confidence was the outcome of the Russian Revolution, or rather of the Bolshevik *coup d'état* that diverted the Russian Revolution from its historic purpose. Coming almost simultaneously with the Balfour Declaration, the Revolution cut off millions of traditionalist Jews from participation in Jewish history. As it was, the contingent of Russian Jewry that got out in time laid the foundations on which most of Israel has risen; it determined the character of the structure and is only now being replaced by a new generation. Chaim Weizmann, David Ben-Gurion, Berel Katzenelenson, Menachem Mendel Ussishkin, Shmarya Levin, Zalman Shazar, Golda Meir, Levi Eshkol, some living, some dead, some remembered, some forgotten, are a small part of the roster. Very few names from the Western or Oriental Jewries appear side by side with them. But half the reservoir of manpower for the Jewish homeland was frozen in its place by Communist decree.

For all these reasons and others given below, the end of World War I was not followed by a tide of Jewish immigration into Palestine. Less than two thousand Jews entered the country in 1919, and a few more than eight thousand in each subsequent year until 1923. In 1924 there was a tremendous leap to thirty-four thousand, as anti-Semitic pressures were increased in Poland. But again the figures dwindled, and in 1927 the gain of immigration over emigration was three thousand. A land as primitive as Palestine then was could not absorb newcomers easily. The populational base was small; the conditions were trying. Vast sums of money were needed, and rich Jews were ready to give for anything but Palestine. I have painful personal memories of those years, when I sometimes accompanied Dr. Weizmann on his begging expeditions to a Jewry that had not yet awakened to the needs, the possibilities, and the realities of the Jewish homeland.

So the work went forward irregularly, with maddening slowness, with pioneers ready and no funds for land to settle them on, with dissension among Zionists as to method, with fierce opposition in Palestine on the part of the old settlement of pietists, whose dreams of the Redemption were being shattered by a form of realization that to them was blasphemy. When I look back, when I recall what a ludicrous and piddling thing the Zionist movement was in the eyes of the world, and how unperceptive most Jews were, I realize again, with a sense of shock, the inevitability with which Zionism must have been endowed to have reached its present stage.

The unreadiness of the Arabs to accept the Weizmann-Feisal plan has now turned into a ferocious rejection of it. In those days it was largely passive. I am speaking here of the Arabs of Palestine. As we have seen, they outnumbered the Jews by about eight to one. Had there been a deep folk resentment against Jewish immigration, had a genuine national opposition to it arisen, then again the Zionist dream would have had to wait for another occasion. But if the Weizmann-Feisal plan meant nothing to the Arab masses, the threat to their nationalism meant little more. Wherever the contact was made, they got along very well with the Jews. They had found an unexpected market for their fruit and vegetables and fish. Arab villages adjacent to Jewish settlements prospered. Thousands of Arabs immigrated from Transjordan and Syria. Daily I saw streams of Arab farmers and workmen pouring into Jerusalem and Tel Aviv, with a contingent of fishermen in the latter city. Jewish shopkeepers who had not yet learned to speak Hebrew, let alone Arabic, chaffered with them in Yiddish, so that Yiddish-speaking Arabs were added to the world's ethnocultural curiosities.

The Arab leaders describe the process differently: as they see it, the simple Arab masses were being slowly and craftily robbed of their heritage, while they, the leaders, warned and protested, staged demonstrations and called to resistance. If many years passed before the Jewish masses could be activated toward the creation of their homeland, in those same years the Arabs have been activated into the defense of their natural rights. Independently of the claim that the Jews had the right to establish their homeland in Palestine, the merit of the pleas entered by the Arab leaders must be examined in the light of their relationship to the Arab masses. It will become evident from the record that the Arab leaders in Palestine, which almost always means the wealthy Arabs, cooperated with the Jews for the purpose of gain as much as they opposed them for the sake of Arab nationalism. Landowners, moneylenders, the effendi class generally, were happy to profit from Jewish colonization, even though their nationalist feelings were wounded. It will also become evident that the concern of the Arab leaders for the welfare of the masses was, outside the area of a common nationalist sentiment, of even more dubious quality.

Arab resistance to Jewish colonization—that is, the Jewish establishment of the homeland—during those early years has a double interest for us, for it tells us much about the British administration of Palestine as well as about the Arabs.

As to the second, there was actually little evidence of major hostility until 1929. If the events of 1929 perturbed us greatly at the time, in perspective they bear out the claim that the Arab masses, exploited and oppressed for centuries by Turkish rule, were simply glad to be able to breathe more easily. There were only two outbreaks that could be associated with anti-Zionist feelings, one in April 1920, the second in May 1921. (The attack on the far-north border of the colony of Tel Hai, in March 1920, in which Joseph Trumpeldor and five of his comrades were killed, was an act of banditry with no political content.)

The first was confined to Jerusalem and resulted in twelve deaths, six Jewish and six Arab. The second began in Jaffa and spread to other areas. The casualties totaled over three hundred, with forty-eight Arab and forty-seven Jewish deaths. On both occasions the preparations for the riots were open and flagrant: inflammatory sermons in the mosques, wild stories circulated of Jewish atrocities and Jewish plans to destroy shrines—this type of Arab propaganda, and the credulity of the Arab masses, have recently become familiar to the world at large. With ample warning in both instances, the preparation of the administration against the events were half-hearted, its handling of them dilatory.

Concerning the first episode Philip Graves, a British correspondent unsympathetic to the Zionist program, wrote:

> It must be admitted that, if most of the accusations brought by the Zionists against the military

administration as a whole were unfounded, there were cases in which individual officers showed pro-Arab or pan-Arab sympathies. The Arabs, sometimes encouraged, perhaps unwittingly, by such officers, grew more and more petulant.

The second episode speaks for itself. It lasted for over a week when a large British garrison in Palestine could have been despatched at once to the points of unrest. But the ambivalent attitude of the administration or of most of its officials came out with devastating clarity in the riots of 1929.

In his autobiography, published when he was already president of the State of Israel, Weizmann asks:

> Why from the very word 'go' did we have to face the hostility, or at least the frosty neutrality, of Britain's representatives on the spot? . . . Why was it an almost universal rule that such administrators as came out favorably inclined toward us turned against us in a few months? Why, for that matter, was it later an invariable rule that politicians who were enthusiastic for the Jewish homeland during the election forget completely about it if they were returned to office?

The question was rhetorical. The representatives on the spot did not, with very few exceptions, have a dynamic and creative attitude toward the idea of a Jewish homeland. It was too much to expect that they would be gripped by the visionary enthusiasm of the Jews, or even to understand it. Many of them were accustomed to dealing with "natives," and to adjudicate their disputes in a decent spirit of fair play; the Arabs were "natives" to them, but the Jews—especially those now coming in—were obstreperously unnative. They were educated Westerners, and they knew their rights, which the British administrators often thought one-sided. And the truth is that a recognition of these rights, stemming from an acceptance of the great philosophy of the Return, still has to penetrate to much of the world today.

If this was not enough, there were also British imperial interests to consider. The Balfour Declaration had at its issuance seemed to coincide with them; it did so less and less as time went on. The Arabs were, after all, more important than the Jews, and until the Balfour Declaration could be gotten rid of, as it was finally, one had to manage somehow. A dual policy of fulfillment and frustration played Arabs against Jews, and Jews against Arabs in truncated Palestine. Until its open repudiation, the promise of the Balfour Declaration was often kept to the eye and broken to the heart. This was not always intentional; it simply arose from the discomforts of an unusual and unwelcome political situation.

Still, for eight years after 1921 the land had rest. This was a decisive period in the growth of the Jewish homeland. The foundations were laid of the spirit and institutions that give Israel its character: the *kibbutzim* (collective colonies), *the moshavei ovdim* (cooperative colonies), the labor movement, the educational system, the social services, the democratic framework of government under a National Council (*Vaad Leumi*), which unfolded at the right moment into the Knesset or Parliament. Between my visits of 1924 and 1929 the *Yishuv* (Jewish settlement) had undergone an inner transformation. It had clearly become the State in the making.

In the matter of learning the principles of self-government, the Arabs of Palestine were in a more favorable position than those of any other country. The leaders turned down the opportunity. In 1922 they were offered a "Legislative Council" to be composed of twelve Arabs (nine Moslem and three Christian), three Jews (all elected by popular vote), and three members of the administration. With most of the administration lukewarm, to say the least, on the question of the Jewish homeland, the Legislative Council would have been a powerful weapon in the hands of the Arabs. But they would have nothing to do with it unless the government first abrogated the Balfour Declaration. This intransigeance has been a permanent feature of the Arab leadership; the less it succeeded the more rigid it became, and it still stands in the way of a fruitful Arab-Jewish accommodation.

The Zionists disliked the idea of the Legislative Council intensely, but they accepted it. They could not bring themselves to oppose a measure so obviously consonant with the principles of democracy. Some of them hoped that if the Arab masses were given a voice they would protect the benefits they were reaping from Jewish immigration. They believed then, as they do still, that the interests of the Arab leaders and those of the Arab masses were diametrically opposed, and time would make this truth obvious to the Arab masses. It was possible that the proposed Legislative Council, with all its dangers, would finally lead to an understanding between Arabs and Jews. This may have been the very reason, certainly one of the reasons, that made the Arab leaders reject it.

There had been a fleeting moment when an overall Arab leadership had risen to a larger view of its relationship to the Arab masses. Had it survived, in the local leadership, the partition of Syria and the excision of Transjordan from Palestine, the Zionist hope could have found bloodless fulfillment even in truncated Palestine. Even within that diminished area a peaceful sifting of the Arab and Jewish populations could have taken place, with a Jewish state rising beside an Arab state. Many Zionists advocated a single binational state. Of course the Arab leadership would not hear of it. Thus what should have been a cooperative enterprise became a contest of wills, and the snarl of problems thickened until the Arab leadership felt driven to cut through it with the sword.

In the contest of wills the Jews, a minority, had the advantage because they were moved by a great ideal and, more significantly, because they were a close-knit, democratic group, with a leadership sprung from the masses and at one with them. When in 1930 I made my own extensive researches among the Arabs, I was staggered by the contrast between the self-rule implicitly practiced by the Jews, and the absence of it implicitly accepted by the Arabs. I had never come in contact with the phenomenon before. Tel Aviv, the all-Jewish city, with a population of 28,500, had an electoral roll of 12,973; in Nablus, all-Arab, the corresponding figures were 15,947 and 928; in Hebron 18,700 and 860; in Gaza 17,480 and 560; and thus throughout all the Arab towns, the proportion of voters to population ranging from one in thirty to one in eleven, with an average of one in twenty. The masses of the Arabs had no political life, and not even the illusion of it, which they got later.

On the land, the lot of the fellahin, or peasants, who constituted the large majority of the population, was miserable in the extreme. They were for the most part share croppers, and the condition of the landowning fellah in the grip of the moneylender was not much better. Only in areas adjacent to Jewish settlements had life begun to rise above its ancient Asiatic level. It was upon these fellahin and upon the equally oppressed workers in the cities that the Arab leadership called to repel the Jewish invaders.

As long as the leadership played on a mixture of motives—patriotism, self-interest, religion—it evoked, as we have seen, comparatively little response. But in 1929 it focused entirely on the religious motive, and this time it was more effective. The riots of that year call for closer attention on several grounds. They were the beginning of mass action on the part of the Arabs; they revealed an Arab capacity for wild, indiscriminate murder; they confirmed the Arab leadership in a policy of violence as the only solution of the Arab-Jewish problem; they alerted the Jews to the greater need for military preparedness; and they brought into clearer view the indecisions and ambivalences of the British administration.

The focus of attention was the Wailing Wall (or, as the Jews call it, the Western Wall) in Jerusalem, the last vestige of the Second Temple, destroyed by the Romans in the year 70. Occupying the same site as the First Temple, Solomon's, it was to religious Jews the most sacred spot in the world, to secular Jews, a deeply moving reminder of one-time national liberty. On this spot fervent services were held on the Jewish High Holy Days, the New Year and the Day of Atonement, and as long as the British mandate lasted the Jews had free access to it. But the spot was also sacred to the Moslems, for from here Mahomet had made his ascent to heaven on *el Burak*.

Until 1922 or 1923 it had been the custom of pious Jews to bring into the narrow alley before the Wall a portable screen to divide the male from the female worshippers on the High Holidays. For some reason the custom lapsed until 1928, when it was revived, and the incident was seized by the Arabs as evidence of Jewish intention to take over the area.

The agitation simmered for a year, then, some weeks before the New Year, 1929, Arabs turned the *cul de sac* before the Wall into a public thoroughfare by breaking a door into one of the houses at the dead end of the alley, so that Arabs were continually passing through, disrupting the services. Protest and counterprotest, incident and counterincident followed, until a tremendous uproar had been created in the country. The Arab leadership kept hammering away at the "Jewish plan to capture the Mosque," and when the

Ninth of Ab (the day of mourning for the Destructions) came round, and Jews again gathered before the Wall for traditional prayers, the agitation rose toward its climax. An Arab proclamation was issued, which read in part:

> On the day of remembrance of destruction of the Temple, Jews gathered to march in a big demonstration with a Zionist banner. . . . They arrived at el Burak and held there speeches which offended Moslem honor. In the markets and el Burak they cursed the Prophet and the Moslem religion . . . the Moslems therefore gathered . . . after prayer . . . and swore unanimously in the name of Allah to defend the honor of the holy places to the last drop of blood.

All over the country groups sprang up pledged to the defense of the Mosque. In one city a committee was founded called "The Knights of el Burak." Tens of thousands of Arabs were thrown into the frenzied belief that a Jewish armed assault on the Mosque was about to take place. When it did not take place the Arab leaders claimed credit for having averted it. The Arab Executive, the then central Arab authority, proudly announced: "El Burak is with God's help intact and will remain forever in Moslem hands"—an anticipation of the many announcements more recently issued by Nasser.

The riots which "averted" the taking over of *el Burak* cost the Jews one hundred thirty-three lives and several hundred wounded. Most, if not all of this could have been prevented if the government had shown a modicum of alertness. The warnings were unmistakable, their duration gave ample time for preparation. Only when the killings were over did the government bring in extra troops from Egypt, where they were within a day's call, and naval ratings from Malta, two days away. Most of the murders were perpetrated far from Jerusalem and the "threatened" Mosque.

In Safed and Hebron, completely defenseless men, women, and children were slaughtered under the most revolting circumstances. In these cities there happened to be no Zionists; Hebron was the center of a yeshivah, or Talmudic college, twenty of whose members were among the victims. Safed, like Hebron, was populated by otherworldly pietists, precisely the kind of Jews the Arabs declared "acceptable."

The conduct of the administration before, during, and after the riots led some Jews to think that it was not altogether sorry to have the Zionists taught a lesson. This is unjust. But there was complete justice in the accusation that its conduct was such that the Arabs could draw that conclusion. One of the mob cries heard frequently those murderous days was: "The government is with us!" Except for a first condemnatory statement issued by the British commissioner, Sir John Chancellor, when he returned from abroad (he was absent during the riots), the administration adopted the attitude that these were not bloodthirsty attacks by Arabs on Jews; they were "disturbances," in which no culprits were named. And this, although of the one hundred sixteen Arab deaths all but six were due to belated police action—which is perhaps not altogether creditable to the Jews. The Hebrew press raged over the difference between *hitnaplut* (assault) and *hitnagshut* (clash)—the similarity of the Hebrew words giving bitter point to the differences in meaning.

The riots of 1929 were far from what the Arab leadership hoped they would be—a general uprising. Had a solid proportion of the eight hundred thousand Arabs risen against the one hundred sixty thousand Jews the casualties would have run into the thousands. The concentrated appeal to the Arabs' most susceptible emotions, the religious, was planted with vicious cleverness; but only a minority rose to it. What went on in the mind of the majority is hard to say; it was not indifferent to religion; the only reasonable conclusion we can draw is that it simply did not believe its leaders, and it did not believe in a Jewish danger.

Such was the first concerted attempt to destroy the Jewish homeland. It was a failure in the short run as well as in the long. Jewish-Arab relations were soon re-established; buying and selling went on, Arab farmers and fruit growers continued to prosper around Jewish settlements, young Arabs from Jaffa resumed, after a pause, their evening visits to Tel Aviv to get a taste of "European" life. But it was never the same again. The Arab leadership had, in the literal sense, tasted blood; and it had become too keenly conscious that its aspirations were not wholly repugnant to the administration. It had also become convinced that it had found the right method: violence.

During the several months I spent in Palestine before, during, and after the riots of 1929 I found little hatred of the Arabs among the Jews. But there was a growing hatred of the British administration. I believe that the general attitude was best described by the weekly *Ha-poel Ha-Tzair,* in its issue of August 30, when the riots were barely over.

> Since the days of the Crusades no such massacre of Jews in Palestine has occurred. Under barbaric and semi-barbaric regimes, during many centuries and changes of rulership, during periods of political anarchy, no events took place like these, which have taken place under modern, enlightened British rule. . . .
>
> We have no dispute with the Arab nation. It was blindly misled by political agitators, and by agents who circulated lies among the Arabs and stirred up the instincts of robbery and murder. But we have a case against the British government. Its duty was to prevent the disaster, which it could have done if it had not refrained from action. . . . The cynical be-

havior of some of the Palestinian officials raises the suspicion that there were those who wanted the disturbances and had secret motives in desiring them. . . .

Our forefathers wrote elegies on massacres like those of Hebron, Safed, and Motza, and preserved their memory in the tears of the Jewish exile. We will not mourn with broken hearts. We will not be discouraged. On the contrary, our connection with the country will be strengthened and our constructive work stimulated. . . . Our return to this country, and the reconstruction of our national life here, constitute a historic destiny which cannot be undone by cunning officials, malefactors, and rioters. . . . We mourn for the Arab blood which was shed; it was not the blood of the instigators, but of those who followed blindly. We do not desire and we do not seek revenge. But we will not abandon our positions. We shall not give up any part of our right to return in masses to Palestine, to build this country, and to live here our free national life. Let this be known to our Arab neighbors, and let it be known to those who advise them evilly to shed our blood in order that they may, in turn, afterwards shed Arab blood.

6

Toward Deadlock

THE moving spirit in the massacres of 1929 was a religious figure, the grand mufti of Jerusalem, Haj Amin el Husseini. As a very young man, he had taken a leading part in the riots of 1920, and he had been sentenced by the military administration to fifteen years' imprisonment. Sir Herbert Samuel, the first high commissioner, amnestied him and promoted him to the most important religious post in Palestine. Although he was a confirmed Zionist, the English administrator in Sir Herbert followed the policy line. The Zionists were extremely critical; they distrusted Haj Amin; they did not believe he would be won over to moderation by the *douceur*. Still, neither they nor Sir Herbert quite foresaw what he would become: a rabid partisan of Hitler and an advocate of the total annihilation of the Jewish people.

For the moment the grand mufti could be satisfied with his achievement of 1929, for it set into motion a series of reactions adverse to the Zionist cause. The British government had changed; the men who had been the chief architects and supporters of the Balfour Declaration, notably

Churchill, Lloyd George, and Balfour himself, were no longer in office. Ramsay MacDonald was prime minister, and Lord Passfield (formerly Sidney Webb) the Labor peer, was his close adviser. MacDonald was lukewarm about Zionism, Passfield ice cold. Between the two the grand mufti could hope for an effective if not formal reversal of the Balfour Declaration, and he got it—temporarily.

A royal commission of inquiry under an agricultural and settlement expert Sir John Hope Simpson was sent to Palestine in 1930. There had been commissions before, and there were to be commissions after—Palestine was perhaps the most frequently investigated country England ever administered. However, I shall confine my attention to the two most important commissions—the Simpson of 1930, and the Peel of 1936.

Sir John Hope Simpson, after long and careful investigation, concluded that there was not room in Palestine for more than 20,000 additional settlers without crowding out the Arabs. There were by then 850,000 Arabs in Palestine, and 170,000 Jews, a total of slightly more than one million. If we look at the population of the area formerly called Cis-Jordan Palestine, as it was on the eve of the June 1967 war, *and subtract the refugees who were living partly on the UNRWA dole,* we find 2,500,000 Jews and 300,000 Arabs and Druzes in Israel, 800,000 Arabs on the West Bank and 150,000 in the Gaza Strip, a total of 3,750,000, all but the last group living on a higher level of subsistence than in 1930. If it is true that this has been made possible by immense Jewish assistance to Israel, it is also true that Israel has had to spend more money on defending herself than she has received from world Jewry.

How could an experienced agricultural and settlement expert underestimate so appallingly the potentialities of the country? Undoubtedly he could not gauge the determination, resourcefulness, and abilities of the Jews and the irresistible drive of Zionism: this has been the fault that has beset nearly every British administrator and everyone who has not taken the trouble to understand the movement. Simpson tried to be objective. He reported:

> The development which has followed on Jewish immigration during the last nine years has provided additional openings for Arab labour. . . . In many directions Jewish development has meant more work for the Arabs, and it is a fair conclusion that the competition of imported Jewish labor is equalized by those increased opportunities.

But he added that what the Jews had to deal with vis-à-vis the Arabs was not the substantive reality, but what the Arabs *thought,* a reality of another order. The report continues:

> So long as widespread suspicion exists, as it does exist, among the Arab population, that the economic depression, under which they undoubtedly suffer, is largely due to excessive Jewish immigration, *and as long as some grounds exist on which this suspicion may plausibly be represented to be well-founded,* there can be little hope of any improvement in the mutual relations of the two races. . . . Arab unemployment is liable to be used as a political pawn [italics added].

Simpson's opinion may fairly be rephrased thus: "The Jews are benefiting the Arabs, but as long as the Arabs don't think so, the relations between Arabs and Jews will be bad." It is an unobjectionable opinion, although one might ask, "Which Arabs is he talking about?" But the action to which Simpson's opinion moved the British government was from every point of view objectionable. For the action proposed to abrogate, in effect, the Balfour Declaration, by placing the severest restrictions on Jewish immigration, and this was the purport of the Passfield White Paper (as it came to be called) issued by the British government in October 1930. It was objectionable first of all because it was demagogic, for it sacrificed the public good to ignorant clamor; second, it surrendered in a cowardly way to an exhibition of the vilest use of force; third, it repudiated an obligation solemnly assumed before the whole civilized world.

The reaction of the Jews of Palestine and of Zionists everywhere was a furious one, and there was a great stir in England. In the House of Commons, the Opposition launched a massive attack; in the London *Times* (in those days still "The Thunderer"), a letter appeared anticipating the contents of the White Paper and warning against its adoption; it was signed by Balfour, Lloyd George, and General Smuts. The result was a retreat by the government, which first reinterpreted the White Paper with maximum favorability toward the Jews, then abandoned it.

The grand mufti's political success was a brief one, if we consider the ultimate outcome of the Zionist movement, but the harm he inflicted on the country was enduring. In the tumult about the White Paper, Ramsay MacDonald appointed as high commissioner to Palestine a man who will be remembered gratefully by those who have any memory at all of the epoch preceding the Second World War. This was Major-General Sir Arthur Wauchope, under whose administration Jewish immigration into Palestine, which had fallen to four thousand in 1931, and less than ten thousand in 1932, swung up to over thirty thousand in 1933, forty-two thousand in 1934, sixty thousand in 1935. Sir Arthur did, to be sure, have the backing of the government, but "the man on the spot," as the British are fond of pointing out, is a decisive factor, and Sir Arthur was sympathetic and cooperative.

The year 1933 is marked heavily on all calendars, Jewish

and non-Jewish: it was the year Hitler came to power. Still the largest immigration into Palestine was not from Germany but from Poland, which, counting three and a half million Jews against Germany's six hundred thousand, was a reservoir nearly six times as large. But fear was in the hearts of all Jews east of the Rhine. Channels of escape were few and narrow. Palestine's was as broad as the country's means allowed—but these were limited. Between 1931 and 1936 the Jewish homeland took in nearly two hundred thousand Jews. The great majority of these would later have perished in the death camps. Between 1936 and 1945 the whole world did not find room for a like number of refugees.

I must return here to the oft-quoted view that without Hitler Zionism would have had no *raison d'être.* This is like saying that if not for death there would no life insurance companies. Zionism in its reactive as distinguished from its creative aspect anticipated that anti-Semitism would be with us for a long time. It did not foresee, nobody had so venomous an opinion of mankind as to foresee, Hitlerian anti-Semitism in all its application; but discrimination, dispossession, and bloodshed were still to be the portion of Jewish communities in various parts of the world. To call Hitlerian anti-Semitism by itself the *raison d'être* of Zionism is to confuse the jolts of history with its general tendency. (Would to God that we still had our six millions, and a free Russian Jewry, and the Jewish state still in the making!)

The history of those years of growth in Palestine is a fascinating subject of study for anyone interested in the human capactiy to turn adversity into gain through the instrumentality of an ideal. The best plea for Zionism is a knowledge of what it did, but a detailed exposition is impossible here. I cannot do more than make an outline, with occasional pauses on crucial points.

To the unprecedented influx of Jews in the years

1933–5 the Arab leadership responded with a change of strategy. They had failed in their attempt to discourage the Jews; without giving it up they turned on the administration, and from 1933 on waged civil war on two fronts. The old Arab Executive was now overshadowed by the Moslem Supreme Council headed by the grand mufti, whose superior abilities were only to bring greater disaster to the country. But by 1936 he was drawing much encouragement from the turn of events in Europe. The Abyssinian War, the prelude to World War II, was reshaping England's and the world's outlook. The great powers had begun to withdraw into fatally narrow calculations of their individual interests, and Hitler's march into the Rhineland in 1936 precipitated division instead of promoting unity. In that same year, but before Hitler's move, Arabs struck at the Jews and at the Palestine administration with a violence that if not initially as savage as that of 1929, was better organized and more sustained.

It began on April 19 with the murder of six unarmed Jewish workers in Jaffa and spread rapidly through the country. A general strike and boycott was called and lasted, with diminishing effect, for six months. One part of the terror was directed against Arabs who tried to maintain peaceful relations with the Jews, and although the number will never be known it is probable that almost as many Arabs as Jews were killed by the rebels.

The simple people who had, for the first time in their lives, achieved a certain degree of prosperity trading with and working for the Jews, hated the boycott. I was witness to secret midnight transactions at the back of the house where we then lived on the eastern outskirts of Tel Aviv. Arabs came furtively across the field from the adjacent village of Sumael to sell their produce; midway they would be met by Jews; some shots would be fired in the air to simulate a clash, in case any of the mufti's men were about, while goods and money rapidly changed hands. The scene was re-enacted at regular intervals here and on the outskirts of many other Jewish settlements.

The six months' spasm subsided into three years of steadier and more spaced violence. It became a war of attrition. Roads between Jewish settlements were mined, harvests set on fire, orchards uprooted. One thought of the days of Deborah the Prophetess, when "the highways were unoccupied and the travelers walked through byways." In reality, however, the roads were not unoccupied, but travelers had to move in convoy—six buses at a time, with an armored car leading and an armored car bringing up the rear.

This was one of the most heroic periods in pre-state Israel. The Jews were determined not to let the terror slow up the pace of land development and the growth of colonies. The Arab plan was to bring everything to a halt; in the event the work rose to a new high tempo. A new technique was evolved in answer to the challenge. Instead of developing a purchased plot by the old piecemeal method—first a vanguard of a dozen or so, then over the years a slow growth into a substantial settlement—the occupation was made swiftly, overnight, by sixty or seventy *chalutzim*. Within twenty-four hours the prefabricated dining room, dormitory, and surrounding wall were assembled, the tower and searchlight erected. Suddenly the colony was there, never to be moved. The number of colonies founded in the years 1936–9 exceeded the number in any other comparable period of the past.

Harder to bear than the minings, the burnings, and the open attacks were the ambushes and random murders, often of a peculiar beastliness. These were a double threat. They were intended to terrorize the Jews, and in this they failed completely; they were also intended to initiate a spiral of vendettas that would culminate in a mutual mass slaughter and a total deterioration of Jewish morale. In this too they failed, but not as completely.

The Jews were particularly on guard against the second danger, with its objective of total chaos and of an irreparable breech between the Jewish and Arab masses. Self-defense was proper; random reprisal, besides being immoral, would play into the hands of the enemy. (The problem was to reappear later on in the border raids on the State of Israel.) *Havlagah,* self-restraint, patience, endurance, was the policy of the Jewish governing bodies and of the vast majority. But there was a minority that scorned the policy as the kind of softness that would only encourage the Arabs. Its members were drawn mostly from the militant Revisionist Party, which had been negligible in size and influence before 1929 but had since become a factor in the country. A number of random reprisals were carried out. They disgusted most of the Jewish population as much for their stupidity as for their immorality. They were the forerunners of that undisciplined terrorism that was later to plague the *Jewish* revolt against the administration. It is well to note in passing that, characteristically, this terrorism was linked with an anti-labor and generally reactionary social philosophy.

The British administration, under direct attack, reacted energetically. It went so far as to arm some Jews in a body known as *gaffirim,* a kind of supernumerary police. It entrusted the suppression of the armed Arab bands to Orde Wingate—a figure who shines out of that dark period with unforgettable brightness. He trained and led Jewish fighters in the guerrilla war in the hills, and like Lawrence of Arabia he has become a legend. The administration was not comfortable with him, and used him only as long as he was found necessary. But while the administration was thoroughly earnest in its campaign to pacify the country, its long-range policy, formulated in England under darkening skies, was a constant encouragement to the Arab revolt.

Half of the pacification consisted of concessions. In 1936 Jewish immigration was again severely restricted: discouragement and encouragement of the rebels were evenly balanced.

But there was also an immense outside source of encouragement to the Arabs. They had at last found powerful allies in the Western world. Germany and Italy took up their cause as part of the cold war (the phrase had not yet come into use, but is applicable) against England and France. The Arabic-speaking radio station at Bari in southern Italy brought to the Arab leaders the assurance that they no longer stood alone. The association between the Axis and the Arab cause was to grow closer in the years to follow. As Germany passed in her treatment of the Jews from robbery, vandalism, and expulsion to annihilation, the grand mufti prophesied of the time at hand when he would deal with the Jews of Palestine as Hitler was dealing with the Jews of Germany. An old man today (in 1968), and no longer a figure in the Arab world, he left on the Arab mind the imprint of the genocidal bent he acquired from the proponents and practitioners of the Final Solution.

Those were three years of suffocation for the Jews of Europe and the Jewish state in the making. Immigration in 1935 reached, as we have seen, sixty thousand. Between 1936 and 1939 it was restricted to a total of fifty thousand. Those were the years of the Nuremberg laws, of the Crystal Night—the licensed destruction of the synagogues and the Jewish shops in Germany—the billion-mark fine extorted from the Jewish community for the murder of a German official. The gas chambers and the crematoria were still undreamt of, except in the diseased minds of the Nazis.

Britain's policy followed, but was not based upon, the findings of the most thoroughgoing of all the commissions sent out to Palestine, that of Lord Peel. It was composed of a group of men of high ability, and its report makes interesting reading as a model of research and organization. I quote from it the passages that deal with the effects of Jewish colonization on the condition of the Arabs.

> It is difficult [wrote Lord Peel] to detect any deterioration in the condition of the Arab upper class. Landowners have sold substantial pieces of land at a figure far above the price it would have fetched before the [First World] war. . . . In recent transactions mainly Palestinian Arabs have been concerned, and the transactions have been considerable. . . . Partly, no doubt, as the result of land sales, the effendi class has been able to make substantial investments of capital. . . . At least six times more Arab-owned land is now planted with citrus than in 1920. . . . Some of the capital has been directed to building houses for lease or sale to industrial enterprise. . . . In the light of these facts we have no doubt that many Arab landowners have benefitted financially from Jewish immigration. . . . A member of the Arab Higher Committee admitted to us that nowhere in the world were such un-economic land-prices paid as by the Jews in Palestine.

We knew, of course, that we were overpaying wildly, but the Arab landowners, the backers of the Arab national movement, had us by the throat. We were desperate. We had to have land for the pioneers. And now to have to listen to talk of our "expropriation" of the Arabs when we paid through the nose for every inch of land!

The Peel Report turns to the condition of the Arab masses and reaches the same conclusion as the Simpson Report but more emphatically.

> The general beneficent effect of Jewish immigration on Arab welfare is illuminated by the fact that the increase in Arab population is most marked in urban areas affected by Jewish development. . . . We

> are also of the opinion that up till now the Arab cultivator has benefitted on the whole from the work of the British administration and from the presence of Jews in the country. Wages have gone up, the standard of living has improved. . . . Jewish example has done much to improve Arab cultivation, especially citrus.

The Arab population had doubled in less than a generation; it had been almost stationary in other Arab countries. Part of the increase was due to constant, uncontrolled immigration of Arabs who were later to be counted as among the original inhabitants of the country. The Peel Report continues:

> The reclamation and anti-malarial work undertaken by Jewish colonists have benefitted all Arabs in the neighborhood. Institutions founded with Jewish funds primarily to serve the National Home (e.g. the medical services of Hadassah and the *Kupat Cholim* [Workers' Sick Fund]) have also served the Arab population. . . . *The Arab charge that the Jews have obtained too large a proportion of good land cannot be maintained. Much of the land now carrying orange groves was sand dunes or swamp when it was purchased* [italics added].

The Zionists were perpetually being accused of not doing enough for the Arabs. The Jewish National Fund came in for particularly sharp criticism. This remarkable institution, conceived before the Zionist movement had acquired the first foot of land in Palestine, was the expression of a deep and traditional Jewish social outlook. It proposed to buy land as the property in perpetuity of the Jewish people, withdrawn from the market and set aside for lease to Jewish cooperative enterprises. Without such land there would have been neither *kibbutzim* nor *moshavei ovdim*. It has been one of the most powerful economic and moral instruments in the upbuilding of the national home. To criticize it for not extending its principles to the Arabs, when Arabs had no inclination for cooperative enterprises, seems to me unjust. But there is wider ground for rejecting the criticism. The idealistic Jewish National Fund was the greatest single spur to Jewish colonization, itself the source of improvement of the Arab condition. To slow up Jewish colonization was to slow up Arab economic progress.

The same argumentation applies to the criticism of the policy that encouraged Jewish employment of Jewish workers. The Jews were coming to Palestine to build their homeland, and in the process they were bringing wide benefits to the Arabs. In some quarters it was apparently expected of them so to increase the benefit to the Arabs as to obstruct the growth of the Jewish homeland. This was not only an absurd missing of the point of the enterprise; it was a practical contradiction.

Could more have been done for the Arabs within the program of the Zionist movement? No doubt it could, and no doubt criticism would have been just as sharp. But it would be very difficult to find in history another example of the occupation of a country with such beneficial results for the existing population. It seemed to be forgotten everywhere that the Balfour Declaration, having accepted the principle of a national home for the Jewish people, had added the stipulation "that nothing shall be done which may prejudice the civil and religious rights of the existing non-Jewish communities in Palestine." Nothing was said about the Jewish homeland bringing great benefits to the existing non-Jewish communities; that happened to be the effect foreseen with enthusiastic approval by the Zionists and was part of their inspiration.

Thus on the eve of World War II the lines were laid down for the theoretical debate that rages on about Zionism today, three decades later. One side argues vehemently that even if all the foregoing is true, the Arabs do not want to have their condition improved by intruders; they want to be left alone to work out their own destiny. This last phrase has a special appeal; it seems to condense in a few words the essence of freedom. If that freedom amounts to the oppression and exploitation of the Arab people by its leaders, if it means that the Arab people is barred from participation in the general advance of mankind, that is nobody else's business.

But, disregarding the impermissible use of the word "intruders" as applying to the returning Jews, the other side challenges the "right" of any people to remain backward, a drag upon humanity. And even if the Arab peoples were completely isolated from the rest of the world, one cannot remain wholly indifferent to the miseries inflicted on them by their leaders. But the Arab peoples want to be part of the world, even want to be helped by it while working out their own destiny. They ask for help "with no strings attached," and wherever that familiar phrase appears it has only one meaning: that the group in power, which does the asking, wants the *status quo* and, if I may so put it, more of it.

The groups in power in some of the Arab countries today use a language of political and social philosophy quite different from that used by their predecessors of thirty years ago. But if we look behind the words we see the same picture: peoples deceived, misled, kept in ignorance of facts; peoples so deprived of self-rule and of freedom of expression that between what they want and what their leaders say they want there is a huge gap that the world is asked to ignore in the name of freedom. It is this gap (if I may mix a metaphor) that explains the deadlock between Jew and Arab. It was wide in 1939; it is apparently wider today.

7

Repudiation

THE Peel Report made it clear that the Jewish homeland could not have been built without the readiness of the Arab upper class to sell large quantities of land to the Jews. In the tug of war between greed and patriotism, greed was the stronger, even though the patriotism, such as it was, had behind it, pulling in the same direction, the class motive. Thus the Arab upper classes betrayed both themselves and what they called the interests of the Arab people.

The self-betrayal presented a sardonic spectacle. Wealthy Arabs detested Zionism no less for the Jews it was bringing into the country than for the new spirit they were bringing with them. More Jews meant more money, larger investments, a wider market; but they also meant more democracy, more *kibbutzim* and cooperatives, and more social service. Those dreadful pioneers, with their liberationist and socialist programs, their proclamation of the dignity of the simple human being, their subversive organization of Arab workers! (The first Arab labor newspaper, *Itahad el Amel,* was founded with the help of the Jews.) The roads of Palestine were infested with young ardent *chalutzim* who believed in the equality of the sexes and the inalienable right of the workingman to a proper share of this world's good things. The example to the Arab masses enraged the effendis, the muftis, the wealthy employers, and the moneylenders. The land was being polluted. As Musa Kasim Pasha, president of the Arab Executive, put it in a cable to the British government in London as far back as 1929, Palestine was being filled with "Jewish riff-raff introduced from all parts to their [the Arabs'] country to build a non-existing nation."

Not all the wealthy Arabs sold land to the Jews, but those who did shared the philosophy of those who did not. They lamented what they profited from, and contributed to the movement which was to put an end to their profits —an excellent illustration of the Marxian dialectic. They hoped the game would go just so far and no farther, reaching a fine balance between maximum financial returns for them and minimum progress for the Jews and the Arab masses. To keep down the progress of the Jews they contributed heavily to the movement which stirred up the Arab masses against Zionism. In their not too subtle calculations they looked foward to bilking the Jews by an ultimate revolt in which they would repossess themselves of their sold property.

To achieve this end it was necessary first to stop Jewish immigration and to turn the Jews into a minority, which could then be made to dwindle by various means—the grand mufti was already advocating the complete liquidation of the Jewish settlement. By 1939 the prospects seemed to be good. The Peel Commission, reporting in 1937, had come to the conclusion that the British mandate, incorporating the Balfour Declaration, was unworkable. It proposed partition of the country into Jewish and Arab states, and that was the beginning of a series of partition proposals all of which in the end were to prove more unworkable than the mandate.

A great storm was unleashed in the Zionist world, which was divided between the Yea-sayers and the Nay-sayers. The Yea-sayers thought partition better than nothing, the Nay-sayers thought it worse than nothing because it was a mockery of Jewish hopes. The debates were long and bitter; suspended or concealed by the outbreak of World War II they burst forth again upon its termination. But in that interval unimaginable things had happened that gave a new and tragic complexion to the Jewish problem and Zionism.

The Peel recommendation, which allotted to the Jews Haifa, the Valley of Jezreel, and the Plain of Sharon, was never acted on by the British government, which proposed instead, to surrender completely to the Arabs, and to repudiate the Balfour Declaration in principle after having abrogated it in action. For in the years 1936–9 the total number of "legal" immigrants was fifty thousand, less by ten thousand than the number for 1935 alone. There is no reliable record of the number smuggled in "illegally"—that is, in defiance of a lawless law; for the entire period 1934–9 it is estimated at no more than 20,000. But in 1939, after having tried in vain to get the Arabs to meet with the Jews at the conference table, the British government issued the last of its White Papers on Palestine, announcing that it had fulfilled its obligations under the Balfour Declaration. Thereafter it would permit Jewish immigration to proceed for five years at the rate of fifteen thousand a year. Beyond that point immigration would have to have the consent of the Arabs.

The 1939 White Paper was the work of that Chamberlain government which has given such a special and pejorative meaning to the word "appeasement." Even with war approaching, the Paper passed Parliament with the relatively small majority of eighty-nine votes. In the debate, one of the most passionate ever heard in the House of Commons, three related themes were sounded by the Opposition: the betrayal of the Jews, the forsaking of the Arab masses to their destructive leaders, and the jeopardizing of England's honor and safety in the headlong retreat before Hitler and his supporters. It is as much by way of tribute to the better England as in support of my thesis that I quote a small part of the opposition speeches.

Winston Churchill:

> There is much in this White Paper which is alien to the spirit of the Balfour Declaration, but I will not trouble about that. I will select the one point upon which there is plainly a breach and repudiation of the Balfour Declaration—the decision that Jewish immigration can be stopped in five years' time by the Arab majority. This is a plain breach of a solemn obligation. . . . If the Government, with their superior knowledge of our deficiency in armaments which has arisen during their stewardship, really feel too weak to carry out our obligations, and wish to file a petition in moral and physical bankruptcy, that is an argument which, however ignominious, should certainly have weight with this House in these dangerous times. . . . We are now asked to submit—and this is what rankles most with me—to an agitation that is fed with foreign money and ceaselessly inflamed with Nazi and Fascist propaganda. . . .

Herbert Morrison:

> If we do this thing today, we shall have done a thing which is dishonourable to our good name, which is discreditable to our capacity to govern, and which is dangerous to British security, to peace and to the economic interest of the world in general and of our own country.

Sir Archibald Sinclair:

> When I think of the Arab people I want to help, I don't think of those powerful feudal families, of the Mufti and the Nashashibis. I think of the fellahin living by the hundreds of thousands on the land, and living there more prosperously, as the Royal Peel Commission reported to us, than they were before the Jews came to establish their National home. . . . I think of the fellahin, of those people who are working in industry and improving their position, of the villages terrorized by the Mufti and working where they can in close cooperation with the Jews . . .

The White Paper was a great victory for the Arab leaders. They had killed the Balfour Declaration, and the partition plan was seemingly dead with it. But they were looking ahead to something more, the elimination of the Jewish settlement in Palestine. If as reactionaries they were the natural allies of Nazi Germany, their affinity with her was reinforced by her maniacal anti-Semitism.* On general and on special grounds they wanted the Allies defeated. As the war dragged on and the abominations that were being perpetrated on the Jews in German-occupied territory leaked through to the world, the need of the Arab leadership for a German victory became desperate. They were right in anticipating that in the revulsion against Germany's mass slaughter of the Jews the Allies, if victorious, would not tolerate the eviction of the Jews from Palestine. On the contrary—horrible thought!—they might even reverse England's policy, revive the partition plan, and arrange for some Jewish immigration. And there was also a simple calculation: Germany's victory would mean the end of Jewry.

* I shall have to speak of the anti-Semitism of the Arabs, a "Semitic" people. Anti-Semitism has become exclusively associated with hostility to the Jews, and can therefore be applied to the Arabs.

There would be no Jews left to want a Jewish homeland, or support it. The little settlement in Palestine could then be easily disposed of.

The position of the Jews of Palestine during the war can only be described as maddening. Their mortal enemy was Germany, their faithless friend was Germany's enemy. Their schizophrenic situation was aptly described by Ben-Gurion: "We shall fight the war as if there were no White Paper, we shall fight the White Paper as if there were no war." They would do everything in their power to help the Allies, they would do everything in their power to annul the White Paper, and to bring in Jewish refugees in the teeth of British opposition.

Within five days of the declaration of war, the *Vaad Leumi,* the Jewish National Council, called for a supreme effort on behalf of the Allies. Within Palestine close on one hundred thousand men and women enrolled for service. A home guard of twenty thousand prevented the Arabs of Palestine from following the example of the Arabs of Syria and Iraq. The Syrians, on French-mandated territory, endorsed the pull-out of the Vichy government, while Iraq staged a pro-Nazi *coup* in April 1941.

In all fairness, it must be recorded that a small number of Arabs did enroll on the side of the Allies, but in 1942, while the Jewish contingents from Palestine counted twelve thousand on the war fronts, the Arab contingents, from a population more than thirty times as large, numbered less than five thousand. Jewish noncombatant battalions took up front-line positions in the desert west of Egypt and were mentioned in dispatches by General Sir Richard O'Connor, who stated that the first capture of Tobruk would have been impossible without the help of these pioneers. General Wavell's report of them was: "They performed fine work, prominently at Sidi Barrani, Sollum, Fort Capuzzo, Bardia, and Tobruk. Despite frequent bombardment, their morale is excellent. . . . They showed remarkable courage and a splendid spirit of self-sacrifice." Of the Jewish fighting contingent the British officer in charge reported: "Never in my life have I seen such keen and gallant soldiers. I am proud of them." Jews served on the sea, in Eritrea, and in Greece. Of the ten thousand prisoners taken by the Germans in Greece and Crete, 1,023 were Palestinian Jews, four hundred twenty-one Arabs.

And while all this went on, shiploads of Jewish refugees were wandering over the Mediterranean, forbidden to land their human cargoes in Palestine. Some of them landed nevertheless, part to be spirited by the Jews into the interior, part to be caught by the British and—unthinkable as it now sounds—shipped to distant Mauritius. Some never landed; the filthy, leaking, rat-infested boats sank with their cargoes.

"I cannot understand why this course has been taken," said Churchill in the White Paper debate. "I search around for the answer. I warn the Conservative Party that by committing themselves to this lamentable act of default, they will cast our country, and all that it stands for, one more step downwards in its fortunes. . . ." On May 10, 1940, Churchill became prime minister. "At last," he writes in *The Second World War,* "I had authority to give directions over the whole scene." In November 1940 two boats, the *Pacific* and the *Milos* reached Palestine with Jews who had escaped from Nazi-occupied territory. The boats were stopped at Haifa and the refugees transferred to the *Patria* for deportation to Mauritius. On November 25 an explosion on the *Patria* killed two hundred and fifty of the passengers. This frightful incident was the result of a blunder; it had been intended by the men who carried out the assignment under the orders of the Haganah merely to cripple the engines; instead a huge hole was ripped in the side of the boat, sinking it. The responsible body announced to the world that what had taken place had been an act of mass suicide, and this was widely believed. The survivors were taken ashore and still held for deportation until vigorous protests from the United States caused the order to be rescinded. The climax of the tragic story was still to come. Of the fifteen hundred survivors, one hundred fifty men enlisted in the British army.

For five years and three months Churchill continued in "authority to give directions over the whole scene." The *Patria* was but one of many of such incidents during his term of office. One cannot escape the reflection that if fifteen hundred survivors yielded one hundred fifty soldiers in the fight against Hitler—we have just heard about their fighting quality—one hundred thousand Jews would have yielded ten thousand.

Such were the exertions and sufferings of the Jews in the days when the freedom of the world hung in the balance, and when the Arab people were either supine or actively supporting the forces of evil. I point up the contrast partly to bring into relief the reward awaiting the Jews at the hands of England when the war was over; but more relevant to the theme of this chapter is the effect on Arab-Jewish relations. Jews and educated Arabs were equally well informed on the posture of affairs, but saw in a different light. To the Arabs Hitler was a promise, not a menace. That the progress of the world would be arrested for centuries by a Hitler victory was a not unwelcome prospect. The difference in view was, as I have said, a reflection of the differences in the political program and also of the human and social philosophy. The destruction of the Jews and of the Jewish homeland was a parallel action to the drive against human progress; that it did not come off was a bitter disappointment to the Germans and to the Arabs. The Germans have come to terms with it. Not so the Arabs.

There has been much talk about the humiliation of the

Arabs, a subject to which I shall return. We have forgotten the humiliation of the Jews—and for the moment I am speaking only of the Jews of the Jewish homeland. Compelled by circumstances and impelled by inclination to expend themselves generously in the fight against Hitler, they were, after his defeat, to be handed over to his accomplices.

8

Desperation

FOR the twelve years 1936–48 the fortunes of the Jewish homeland fall into three periods: from 1936 to 1939, the Arab revolt, backed by Germany and Italy, concentrated on the arrest of Jewish development in Palestine; from 1939 to 1945, the Jews of Palestine, in what I have called a schizophrenic dilemma, fought with equal determination Germany and the White Paper; from 1945 to 1948, with the war against Germany successfully concluded, the Jews were in open revolt against the British administration: there was only the White Paper to be fought and destroyed.

It was widely expected that with the defeat of Hitler, and appeasement a shameful thing of the past, a brighter prospect would open for the Jewish homeland. Most promising was the change of government in England. Labor was now in power with an astoundingly large majority, and Labor was expected to show a particular sympathy for the progressive character of the Jewish settlement, as contrasted with the social backwardness of the Arab leadership.

On this last point the Zionists suffered one of their most

cruel disillusionments, and it is here that Weizmann's complaint is most tellingly relevant: "Why was it an invariable rule that politicians who were enthusiastic for the Jewish homeland forgot completely about it if they were returned to office?" Lord Passfield, the Laborite, had been honest in his anti-Zionism before he took office; not so Ernest Bevin, the postwar foreign secretary. As a Trades Union Member of Parliament before the war, he had actually helped to defeat the Passfield Paper; now, to the stupefaction of the Zionists, he declared himself unalterably opposed to their program, and his utterances on it were such as to raise a strong suspicion of an anti-Semitic streak in his makeup.

The climate of opinion in the Western world gave the Zionists grounds for hope. Until 1939 Hitlerian anti-Semitism had been regarded among liberal people as a transient phenomenon, a miserable propaganda device. Hitler did not mean the literal annihilation of the Jewish people (today Arabs are explaining that they did not mean the literal destruction of Israel). The illiberals did not care. But after the war a feeling of shame spread among all but the most viciously minded. Now it was remembered how evasive even the liberals had been, how the Jews had been advised to mute their protests, how they had been accused of grossly exaggerated apprehensions, how they had been told, in effect: "Do not scream while the crocodile is devouring you. Perhaps you will sate his appetite, and we shall be spared." Now it was realized that the Jews had been right; the appetite of the crocodile had only been whetted, and the democracies had not been spared.

America was to be a factor of crucial importance for Israel in the postwar years. Those who believe that history is not meaningless will see in this the teleology of Jewish survival. America has been Jewry's anchor to windward, anticipating the storm that broke over the ancient communities of Europe. It is impossible to think of world Jewry or Israel without America's fateful role in them. That America was not concerned with Jewish survival when she opened the gates to hundreds of thousands of East European Jews is irrelevant to the teleological view; so are the mechanics, the zigzags, and the contradictions of the historical operation. From the time of Wilson on, American Presidents have taken an affirmative view of Zionism, as have the majority of leading American politicians. Franklin Roosevelt may have made contradictory promises to Ibn Saud and to Weizmann; the handling of the Sinai war in 1956 by Eisenhower and Dulles may have been unfriendly to Israel; the Jewish vote and the oil interests may have influenced congressmen and senators in opposite directions. The total effect has been a great affirmative intervention on behalf of Israel, and this has been consonant with the general mood and tradition of America. In particular, the pressure exerted by Truman immediately on the close of the war was both an immense encouragement to Israel and a brake on England's destructive policy between 1945 and 1947.

During the war years, and partly as a result of the Holocaust, a change had come over American Jewry, an augury of what was to reveal itself so powerfully in May and June 1967. Wider circles responded to the Zionist cry for a homeland, and on their visits to America during the war years Weizmann and Ben-Gurion found support in hitherto inaccessible quarters. Much of the response was of a purely philanthropic nature, untinged with a sensitivity to the historic foundation of the Zionist idea. Some of it may be described as prudential: hundreds of thousands of Jewish survivors had to be taken out of the death camps and given new homes, and with Palestine ready to receive them the pressure would be eased on other countries. But every kind of support was welcomed by the Zionists, confronted with the appalling turn of events in England.

The struggle between Palestinian Jewry and the British Empire for the control of Palestine could to all appearances have only one outcome—the crushing of the Jewish will and the consequent dissolution of the Jewish settlement. But the appearances did not correspond to the effective forces. What for England was policy was for Palestinian Jewry life and death. In the wide context of England's interests, Palestine and even the good will—anyhow unreliable—of the Arabs were expendable; the Jewish homeland had no context, it was everything. And so the Jews of Palestine resolved to make it impossible for the British to govern the country as long as they tried to enforce the White Paper. And in this the wretchedly armed, numerically small community succeeded.

For the carrying out of such a program the strictest discipline was essential. The Haganah was the official instrument of the resistance. Its policy was one of strikes, destruction of installations, disruption of communications —but no attempts on the lives of British personnel. It was also opposed to uncoordinated sabotage, and above all to acts of terrorism involving bloodshed.

Two dissident groups opposed this program, the Revisionists and the *Lechi* (*Lochamei Cheruth Israel,* the Freedom Fighters). Both—especially the latter—were contemptuous of the "soft" official line taken by the representative body of Palestinian Jewry. They were responsible for some ugly acts, among them the assassination of Lord Moyne and of Folke Bernadotte, the United Nations mediator. In particular Revisionists, who organized their own army, *Etzel* (*Irgun Tzva Leumi,* the National Army Organization) must be held responsible for the revolting incident of Deir Yassin, to be described later; the *Lechi* took a leaf from the Arab book and assassinated a number of Jews it suspected of collaborating with the British. The Haganah has been accused of having acted in complicity with the Revisionists in the anti-British terror, and there may have been points of contact; but it must be remembered that essentially the Revisionists were creating a private, unofficial, and anti-official army, a counterbody to the Haganah, for the purpose —we have strong grounds to suspect—of bringing off a *coup d'état* and taking over the government when a Jewish state was established.

The rivalry between *Etzel* and the Haganah extended to gunrunning, gun-buying from sympathetic or lax or corupt British soldiers and officers, and the bringing in of "illegal" immigrants. Among old-time Zionists the debate still continues as to the relative values of the two branches of the revolt, the Revisionist partisans asserting that while they did not command the means of the official body, their contribution to the defeat of the British was the greater as an inspiration and example. They have, in my opinion, a doubtful case at best. What is not doubtful is the high point of the rivalry. When the state had been established the Revisionists tried to land a shipload of arms; one of the early unhappy acts of the newly established Jewish government was to sink the boat off the shore at Tel Aviv, killing some of the gunrunners.

In the smuggling through of refugees there could be no comparison between the achievements of the Revisionists and the Haganah. The Revisionists gathered funds from small groups in America and elsewhere; the Haganah had wide support and it developed a fierce activity in the buying and chartering of boats and the organizing of transportation. The most famous attempt cannot really be described as a smuggling operation; it was carried out in the light of day, with the world's attention fixed upon it, and its failure was more than offset by the sympathy it aroused for Palestinian Jewry and the damage it did to the British government at home and in Palestine.

This was the *Exodus* incident of the summer of 1947.

The ship, a leaky ferry originally named the *President Warfield,* arrived at Haifa with forty-five hundred refugees. The administration, on instructions from London, would not let them land. They were loaded onto British ships and sent back to their point of embarkation in southern France. But the refugees refused to leave the boats there. They wound up in the country from which most of them had originally fled—Germany. It should be pointed out that the final port they were directed to, Hamburg, was now in the British zone of occupation, and therefore "returned to Germany" was not exactly what the phrase seemed to imply. That did not matter. The impression created on the public by this stupid act of Bevin's was deep and lasting.

Those were hard and cruel days in Palestine. The Jewish community seemed to be on the point of civil war even when it was trying to direct all its energies toward the defeat of the administration. I can testify from personal observation during the period to the general loathing inspired by the acts of the Revisionists and the *Lechi.* All the fine moral temper that had made possible the social achievements of the Zionists rose in protest. When the terrorists hanged two British sergeants, and booby-trapped one of the bodies as a reprisal for the execution of three of their numbers for participating in an attack on the jail in Acre, a shudder went through the community. What was happening to the Zionist ideal?

One can spare a little sympathy at this distance for the British administration. The rank and file of the army could not be expected to distinguish between the Haganah and the terrorists, and when Arab attacks on Jews took place, the soldiers often looked the other way. I quote the report for that period of *The Survey of International Affairs,* a product of Chatham House under the editorship of Arnold J. Toynbee, both notoriously anti-Zionist:

> The Zionists complained that the British security forces were not doing enough to protect Jewish lives and property. Almost certainly they were now doing less than their strict duty, for the temper of the British soldiers had been affected by the fact that they had lost 127 killed and 331 wounded at the hands of Jewish terrorists between the end of the Second World War and 20 October, 1947.

But "looked the other way" and "less than their strict duty" are understatements. There were many cases of brutality perpetrated by soldiers against innocent Jews.

On February 14, 1947, Britain gave up. This is the only interpretation that can be placed on her decision to relinquish the mandate and turn it over to the United Nations. For her the Zionist experiment was over. It would be pleasant to say that she bowed out gracefully, in the best tradition of sportsmanship, but it would not be truthful. When the UN appointed its Special Committee on Palestine, Great Britain did not cooperate; and up to the time when she withdrew her forces she lent her fading authority to the Arab cause.

The United Nations Special Committee was appointed in May 1947. It held its first meeting in New York, and was assured by Secretary-General Trygve Lie that "you are entitled to be confident that, in the event it should be necessary, the Security Council will assume the full measure of responsibility in implementation of the Assembly's resolution." The resolution was to be based on findings of the Committee. The promise of the Secretary-General of the United Nations was taken very seriously at the time, and UNSCOP proceeded to Palestine in June, arriving there as the three-sided Zionist-British-Arab struggle was rising to a climax.

Eleven countries were represented on UNSCOP: Australia, Canada, Czechoslovakia, Guatemala, India, Iran, the

Netherlands, Peru, Sweden, Uruguay, and Yugoslavia. Throughout the summer of 1947 its members investigated earnestly, listened to countless witnesses and experts, traveled in the fiery heat to various sections of the country, and waited in vain for an Arab spokesman to appear. All around them the fighting went on, like an admonition. In September UNSCOP was ready with its report, to which a majority of the members appended their signatures.

The recommendations of UNSCOP are too well known to need detailed exposition here. It is enough to recall that the one quarter left of the territory originally meant for the Jewish homeland was sliced up in a fantastic effort to find a viable section to contain a Jewish majority.* The boundaries wandered along extended lines that seemed almost designed to invite attack. The new Jewish state was to be a wasp-waisted crazy quilt, its middle ten miles wide—on the east the new Arab state, on the west the Mediterranean. Still, it was less niggardly than the division recommended by the Peel Commission, and much less so than another recommended by a subsequent commission, the Woodhead, in 1948. It fell short, as might be expected, of the division proposed by the Zionists. It excluded the Jews from some of their most cherished historical and religious sites. It set Jerusalem apart for internationalization. And still, when it was adopted in the United Nations General Assembly on November 29, 1947, by a vote of thirty-three to thirteen, a great wave of rejoicing went through the Jewish homeland and through most of the Jewish world.

Great Britain abstained from the voting, but Russia voted in favor. For what they are worth, some of the words of the Russian representative, Andrei Gromyko, should be recalled.

> The Union of Soviet Socialist Republics, as everyone knows, has no direct material or other interests

* See map, page 4.

in Palestine. It is interested in the question of Palestine because it . . . bears a special responsibility for the maintenance of international peace. . . . The experience gained from the study of the Palestinian question . . . has shown that Jews and Arabs are unable to live together within the boundaries of a single state. The logical conclusion followed that, if these two peoples inhabit Palestine, *both of which have deeply rooted historical ties with the land* . . . there is no alternative but to create, in the place of one country, two States. . . . The U.S.S.R. delegation holds that this decision corresponds to the fundamental national interests of both peoples. . . . The representatives of the Arab states claim that the partition of Palestine would be an historical injustice. But this view of the case is unacceptable if only because, after all, the Jewish people *has been closely linked with Palestine for a considerable period of history* [italics added].

The historical connection of the Jewish people with Palestine is mentioned twice in Gromyko's address. Weizmann records that he had the utmost difficulty in getting this admission into the preamble to the mandate which ratified the Balfour Declaration. He had suggested: "Recognizing the historic rights of the Jewish people to Palestine," and the British would not have it. Finally the compromise phrasing was agreed on: "Recognizing the Jewish historical connection with Palestine." Weizmann writes: "I confess that for me this was the most important part of the Mandate. I felt instinctively that the other provisions of the Mandate might remain a dead letter . . . but not this recognition of the Jewish claim." One wonders why Gromyko so easily granted what Weizmann had to fight for so strenuously in the League of Nations. The gesture was completely gratuitous, and it had nothing to do with Russia's intentions which were, clearly, to get England out of Palestine. The only answer I can think of is that when the Russians take up a position it has to be whole hog, absolutely, with every possible argument in its favor and dissension automatically precluded. They do this because they are able without embarrassment to take up the opposite position with the same gusto and absoluteness.

That they can do this successfully is proved by the fact that many Jews took Gromyko's speech seriously, and were touched by it. It added to their happiness. Russia too realized that the Jewish state was not an upstart historically. It was here once more after an interval of two millennia, the place where an independent Jewish people on its soil would be free to develop according to its character and its abilities, free to demonstrate its capacity to contribute to the modern world, free, above all, from the pressures and condescensions of even the friendliest environment. As for the smallness of the territory, they would try again to make do, as they had after the first huge excision of Transjordan. They had shown that they could triple and quadruple the productivity of the land. The now barren Negev had in ancient days supported a large population; it should do so again. The ancient world had not known the wonders of modern industry, yet Palestine in the days of the Second Commonwealth had supported a population of nearly three million. One half of Palestine could support more than that number today.

Such were the hopes in the Jewish homeland despite the shrunken area and the snakelike borders, and despite the threats and assaults of the Arabs. But between the passing of the resolution by the UN and the proclamation of the Jewish state on May 14, 1948, much happened to upset these hopes and the hopes the world had built on the United Nations.

The Arabs said No! The United Nations be damned. There was not to be a Jewish state even in that section of

Palestine where the Jews were in a majority. They defied the United Nations and prepared to destroy the nascent Jewish state by force of arms. Within that part of Palestine which had been assigned for a new Arab state, as within the area of the Jewish state-to-be, England's mandatory writ still ran. She was still responsible for the maintenance of the peace in both areas; but when surrounding Arab states began to mobilize their forces within the non-Jewish area, she did not intervene. A "Palestine Liberation Army" was recruited and was joined by contingents from Syria and Iraq. Egypt concentrated a force at Gaza. Most formidable of all was Jordan's Arab Legion, trained by Sir John Glubb (Glubb Pasha). *The Survey of International Affairs* reports: "The Arab forces were based, with a large measure of British tolerance, on localities within the territory assigned to the [new] Arab State by the resolution on Partition." Britain was going to see to it that there was a fair fight between fledgling Israel and the five Arab states surrounding her.

What a singular role the Jewish state was called upon to fill while still a-borning! The promise of the Secretary-General of the UN that "the Security Council assumes the full measure of responsibility in implementation of the Assembly's resolution" took on a sardonic meaning. The full measure of responsibility was carried by the state that was not yet in existence when the promise was made. Of the registered members of the UN not one came forward to carry a share of the responsibility. The one member that could have made at least a negative contribution by forbidding the mobilization of armies on the territory it still administered, connived with the contumacious members preparing to destroy the state-to-be and the UN.

The Jews of the homeland fought alone, as they were to fight alone nineteen years later. They fought for their lives but, paradoxically, not for the reputation of the UN; for, surviving, they were a standing reproach to it. Dead, they would have been forgotten. What did not survive was the impossible partition plan. No new Arab state came into existence. The emirate of Jordan moved in and swallowed up the territory. No internationalized Jerusalem came into existence. The Jewish forces failed on this point, and thenceforth the Old City, with its precious Western Wall, and its many ancient synagogues, was closed to them. They could not set foot in it any more than in the days of Roman Hadrian.

9

The Arab Refugees

(1)

WHAT the Arabs said to the UN in 1947 was: "We withdraw the Palestine problem from your competence," and they proceeded to make good the statement by their actions. Short of expelling the Arabs, the answer of the UN should have been: "In that case we will keep our hands off, and you can settle your problems with the Jews in direct negotiations." This is the sensible and logical—and the only possible—position taken by Israel. But the Arabs want it both ways. The Palestine problem is not within the competence of the UN, but the UN is to be used by the Arabs whenever they think they can score a point with its help. And the UN has stultified itself for twenty years by lending itself to this ploy.

What the Arabs did further in 1947–8 was to create the Arab refugee problem. It will be helpful to consider the first phase separately before we pass to the second, post June 1967.

When the UN Partition Resolution was passed in November 1947 there was in the territory assigned to the Jewish state a slight majority of Jews over Arabs, approximately six hundred fifty thousand to six hundred thousand. It was the intention of the Jews to widen that margin by bringing in hundreds of thousands of survivors from Europe and as many Jews as possible from Arab countries. The creation of the Jewish state had been authorized for the purpose of taking care of Jewish refugees, and the condition of Jews in the Arab countries was an impossible one. Ultimately, the number of Jews taken in from Arab countries rose to half a million, equal to the number which the Arabs by their folly caused to be displaced from the Jewish state. What took place in fact was an aborted exchange of populations, Israel admitting the Jewish refugees, the Arab states closing their doors to the Arab refugees.

We can now see with greater clarity how the breakup of the Greater Syria, which was the basis of the Weizmann-Feisal plan, and the arbitrary cutting away of Palestinian Transjordan from the application of the Balfour Declaration, have bedeviled the issues. The physical impairment of the original plans has also led to an impairment of the truth. Suddenly the false thesis was established that if a Cis-Jordan Palestine Arab moved into Jordan or Syria he was going into exile, he was being deprived of his nationalist base. The thesis was equally false with regard to Iraq or Lebanon or Egypt. The similarity of faith, language, tradition, social forms, living conditions (allowing for provincial differences) disappeared from the public view. Overnight the idea of a specific Arab-Palestinian nationalism sprang up out of a purely provincial geographic term.

This is not to deny that Arab leaders in Palestine felt themselves entitled to become the rulers of the country and proclaim a Palestinian nationality. What is emphatically denied is their claim that the masses they exploited and spoke for felt themselves to be of Palestinian nationality, felt that their Arabism (for want of a better term) was attached to the small area comprised by the 10,000 square miles of Cis-Jordan Palestine out of the 44,000 comprising all of Palestine, or the roughly 120,000 comprising Greater Syria, or for that matter, the much larger area comprising the other Arab countries I have mentioned.

There is meaningful psychological and spiritual, if not ethnic, substance in the assertion: "I am an Arab." The assertion: "I am a Syrian," or Jordanian, or Iraqi, has none. "I am an Egyptian" does have some, but Egypt began a national development more than a hundred years ago with Mohammed Ali. I felt Egyptian-Arab nationalism among the upper classes in my visits to Egypt thirty and forty years ago; I also felt the Egyptians' indifference to, or rather contempt for, the Palestinian Arab.

Syria, Iraq, Jordan are not yet nationalisms in the European sense. They are more in the nature of group interests, independent governmental organizations with separate economic and political programs. Their rivalries take precedence over their common Arab nationalism, just as the rivalries of European countries take precedence over their common feeling of Europeanism. But there is this crucial difference: Europeanism is the weaker feeling in Europe, while local nationalisms are deep-rooted and strong; Arab nationalism is the stronger sentiment while local nationalisms hardly exist. But the common Arab nationalism is not strong enough to overcome regional ambitions. What I have said about Syria, Iraq, and Palestine applies in varying degrees to Saudi Arabia, Yemen, and the sheikhdoms scattered along the periphery of the Arabian peninsula. The one common political bond is negative—their enmity toward Israel.

We should remember, however, that a common enmity does not promote common bonds of friendship. On the contrary, its concealment of old rivalries—where such concealment takes place—banks their fires, which burst out all the more fiercely when the reason for concealment is removed (cf. the Grand Alliance that fought Nazi Germany). It is frequently said that the common enmity to Israel is the great promoter of Arab unity. It is in fact the temporary, and extremely imperfect, concealer of Arab disunity. When unity comes to the Arab peoples—a desirable consummation—it will have to be on a very different basis. Fortunately a common enmity, however necessary it may be or seem to be strategically at a certain period, is in itself barren and ultimately exhausting; despite the most furious protestations, it will die much more easily than a bond arising from affirmative interests.

(II)

Before entering on the history of the Arab refugee problem, I think it proper to make some general observations.

What I have said regarding the weakness of localized Arab nationalisms must not be taken as excluding certain universal human sensitivities. Poor and exploited though he may be, the Arab fellah can love the plot of land that he and his ancestors have cultivated for centuries. He can be deeply attached to the familiar landscape, the village, the local mosque, the cemetery where his ancestors lie buried. If, in spite of this attachment, he chooses to move, and this happens often, it is a wrench. The largest number have not chosen to move, and that they should be forced to move is always a tragedy, just as hard to bear when it is caused by a fellow Arab as when it is caused by a stranger.

The love of the Jewish people for its ancient homeland is of a different kind from that of the Arab. Its potency was hitherto known only to Jews—and not to all of them. Only a great and potent love could have created Israel. Homelessness, oppression, humiliation cannot explain it. Though the majority of Jews have come to Israel because they had nowhere else to go, the foundations were laid by Jews who were drawn to it by an overwhelming passion. I have described in other books the unbelievable hardships they endured in those far-off days when with a little patience they could have found an outlet for their immense abilities in the Western world. The painful transformation they wrought in themselves from ghetto and *shtetl* dwellers, children of peddlers or merchants or professionals, into peasants or laborers was paralleled by the transformation they wrought on a land wasted and denuded by immemorial misrule, apathy, and corruption. What they did here Jews have never done in any of the colonization enterprises they have attempted in other parts of the world. These have withered away because their only motivation was the will to escape from bondage, from insecurity, and from the sordidness of a marginal mercantile existence. Israel has made its brilliant record because the decisive motivation was the love for the land transmitted without diminution across sixty generations.

That majority which came only because it had nowhere else to go discovered after a time, and somewhat to its astonishment, that this is what it had really needed. For it discovered its roots; and it discovered that it was not going out of the modern world, but into one of its liveliest and most significant sectors. If the immigration bars were to be dropped today in the affluent lands of the West, a certain proportion of the Israeli population would undoubtedly avail itself of the opportunity; it would include not only some of the recent refugee arrivals, but children of the original pioneers too. But Israel as a whole is immovably rooted, and the rediscovery of the roots proceeds from year to year with deepening effect. One of the most moving indications of the reconnection with the far-off past is the excitement aroused by archeological findings. Thousands of quite unscholarly people—waiters, taxi drivers, tailors, farmers, factory workers

—have become amateur experts on potsherds, figurines, manuscripts, artifacts, and ruins dating back to Biblical times, and tens of thousands read with intelligent interest of the excavations at Masada, Caesarea, and elsewhere. It is an emotional interest. It brings up a cry from the heart: "This land is ours!" And continually, as Hebrew works its way into widening areas of newcomers, the Bible itself becomes once more the Book of the People. Independently of the formal or ritualistic expression of religious feeling, the spiritual power of the unique and manifold statement of man's destiny penetrates to all sections of the population, and from it comes an answering cry: "This land is yours!"

But let it be noted that the cry refers *only* to Cis-Jordan Palestine. Where an attachment of the same kind exists among the Arabs, it is spread over the whole vast territory of the Arab states.

(III)

I TURN ONCE MORE to *The Survey of International Affairs*:

> The beginning of the Arab mass flight went back to an early stage in the Arab Jewish fighting. As early as January 1948 the High Commissioner had confirmed a "steady exodus" of Arab middle-class families who could afford to leave the country, taking with them cars and considerable quantities of goods.

This was four months before Israel declared her independence, that is, four months before the Arab armies invaded her territory. Who were these middle-class families that could afford to leave the territory and did? They were the backbone of the Arab resistance, its planners and financial supporters.

These leaders of the Arab masses did not steal away unobserved, of course. The roads they took led through Arab villages, under the eyes of those who could not make so comfortable a flight. But the example was infectious, and was soon followed by tens of thousands, on donkey, or on foot, with the pitiful belongings of the poor on the backs of old and young. On August 12, 1948, Sir John Glubb, the lifelong Arab partisan, wrote in the *Daily Mail* of London: "The Arab civilians panicked and fled ignominiously. Villages were frequently abandoned before they were threatened by the progress of the war."

It was not enough for the Arab leaders to get out of the way of danger. They urged the example upon the masses. *The Survey of International Affairs* affirms: "A . . . Zionist assertion that the Higher Arab Committee had 'called on the Arab population to leave the country en masse' should be treated with reserve." But five years after the events the Jordan daily *Al Difad,* speaking for the refugees, said: "The Arab government told us: 'Get out so that we can get in.' So we got out but they did not get in."

A cold reading of the facts leaves the picture thus: the Arab masses in their panic lent themselves to the military plans of the Arab leadership. One must pity the Arab masses, but what of the Jews? They were fighting for their lives, and *their* civilian masses could not get out of the way of the fighting. It would have been natural for the Jews to be filled with blind rage against the Arab masses, and yet the truth is that in many instances they tried to stop the Arab flight. *The Survey* reads:

> The Arab irregulars' use of conveniently situated Arab villages as bases for attacks on Jewish localities, and the consequent Jewish reprisals against such villages, had caused a considerable flight from villages on the fringe of Jewish territories to safer places . . . but there can be no question that the publicity which the Arab press and radio gave to the

> massacre at Deir Yassin for the purpose of attracting sympathy greatly accelerated the demoralization and flight of the non-combatant Arabs. At this stage of the fighting the Jewish attitude to the Arab flight was ambiguous, since, while there is clear evidence that the civil authorities at Haifa tried to tranquilize the population, the Jewish combattants there and elsewhere made skilful use of psychological warfare to break their opponents' morale. At a later stage the Israeli armed forces did not confine their pressure on the Arab population to playing on their fears. They forcibly expelled them . . .

Several points call for comment. The word "reprisal" is here grossly misused, as it so often has been in connection with the Arab-Jewish conflict. If the Arab village A is being used as a base for attacks on the Jews, and an attack is made on the Arab village B, that is a reprisal; but an attack on the Arab village A is not a reprisal, it is self-defense. Such, according to Revisionist spokesmen, was the case with the village of Deir Yassin. But even if the Revisionist's claim is false, this case, *the only one of its kind in the whole of Israel's War of Independence,* has been lifted out by Arab propaganda to characterize the attitude of the Jews.

The action against Deir Yassin was carried not by the establishment forces, that is, the Haganah, but by the dissident Irgun and Lechi, and against the wishes of the Haganah. According to the accounts of the Revisionists, the villagers were repeatedly warned to remove the women and children before the attack was launched. The warnings were unheeded, and in the fighting large numbers of women and children were killed. The Arabs placed the number at three hundred, but the total for men, women, and children was about one hundred and fifty. It was a disgraceful incident; Deir Yassin should not have been attacked under the circumstances, whatever the provocation, if any. There was a great outcry among the Jews; the establishment condemned it in the severest terms and issued a statement of profound regrets and apologies. The old poisonous controversy between Haganah and the dissidents reached here its highest point before the gunrunning incident and the sinking of the Revisionist ship.

Arab strategy called for an evacuation of the Arab civilian population, leaving the field clear for military action. Deir Yassin was seized upon as a windfall. Horrible as the incident was, it was embellished by Arab propaganda with grotesque and sickening details. The Arabs, already in a ferment of flight, were told that the survivors of Deir Yassin were paraded through the streets of Jewish Jerusalem and mocked at and spat upon. Little wonder that, as *The Survey* confirms, the flight was greatly accelerated. All these facts must be borne in mind when the question is asked: "Who created the Arab refugee problem in 1947–8?"

I have quoted largely from *The Survey* because it cannot be suspected of a pro-Zionist bias. Actually the bias is anti-Zionist and anti-Semitic. In this report appears, for the first time as far as I know, the equating of the Jews with the Nazis, developed by Arnold J. Toynbee in his *Study of History* and turned more recently into standard propaganda by Communists and Arabs. In an earlier account *The Survey* offers the statement: "Zionists were apt to compare the discrimination against Jews in the Diaspora with that against 'colored people,' but once in their 'ancient homeland' they themselves behaved as a *Herrenvolk*."

Toynbee's mammoth *Study of History* is little read now, and even less respected in the learned world, but his development of the noisome suggestion "Zionism equals Nazism" has filtered through to the popular level—all of him that the public remembers, without remembering its origin. He wrote:

> The evil deeds committed by the Zionist Jews against the Palestinian Arabs that were comparable to the crimes committed by the Nazis against the Jews were the massacre of men, women, and children at Deir Yassin on the 9th April, 1948. . . . On the morrow of a persecution in Europe in which they had been the victims of the worst atrocities ever known to have been suffered by Jews or indeed by other human beings, the Jews' immediate reaction to their own experience was to become persecutors in their turn for the first time since 135 A.D. —and this at the first opportunity that had arisen for them to inflict on other human beings *who had done the Jews no injury* [italics added], but who happened to be weaker than they were, some of the wrongs and sufferings that had been inflicted on the Jews by their many Western Gentile persecutors during the intervening seventeen centuries.

And again: "On the Day of Judgment the gravest crime standing to the German Nationalist Socialists' account might be, not that they had exterminated a majority of the Western Jews, but that they had caused the remnant of Jewry to stumble."

It is hard to get at the meaning of these sanctimonious closing sentiments. My best guess is: "The worst feature of the slaughter of six million Jews by the Nazis is that it caused a small dissident group of Zionists in Palestine to commit a horrible crime." Now the most remarkable feature of the Nazi slaughter of six million Jews, added to the world's cruel indifference—not to speak of the seventeen centuries of persecution they have endured—is that the Jews have not been reduced to an irreclaimable condition of rancor and vengefulness. Such is their spiritual resilience that they have remained a people with a high record of generous and liberal thought and action. To demand of them what is demanded of no other people, that they should be completely free from human faults, that not the smallest proportion of them should "stumble" is, under the circumstances, a peculiar kind of cynicism.

But this cynicism invests all of the criticism which is leveled at the Jews and at Israel in respect of the Arab refugee problem. First, taken as a whole, the charge that the Jews drove the Arabs out of the Jewish state is one of the Big Lies of modern history. Second, it seems to have been expected of the Jews that they conduct a war of survival in a spirit of unblemished saintliness. Third, and this has been a continuous theme for the past twenty years, they must treat the Arab refugee problem without regard to their own safety.

The intractability of the problem in its first phase—that is, until the war of June 1967—lay in its exploitation by the defeated Arab countries. It was not the intention of the Arab leaders that the refugees should return as peaceful—let alone loyal—citizens of the Jewish state. For they never recognized, still do not recognize, its existence. They speak only of "occupied Palestine." The refugees were to return as a gigantic fifth column. To add to their wretchedness, and to keep them in a condition of sustained and mounting fury, they were compelled to remain where they were, resettlement in the Arab states denied them, eating the sour bread of international charity washed down with drafts of hatred brewed locally. If Israel would not admit them freely, to her own undoing, they would reenter Palestine anyhow, in the wake of the conquering armies of their brothers, when Israel would be swept into the sea. Meanwhile they were to provide raiders and killers as the heralds of the liberation.

The demand for the readmission of the refugees was part of a simple overall formula which also applied to the question of frontier lines. It ran—and runs—thus: "Our purpose is to destroy the Jewish state. If we attack, and are thrown back, the Israelis must return to their original positions.

This is to be repeated until we have achieved our purpose." The simplicity of the formula gave it wide appeal among "neutrals" who could not see why Israel should seek safer frontier lines after having been attacked and why the refugees should not be readmitted. The first was cried down as "annexationism," the second as contrary to humanitarianism.

When one compares the treatment meted out to the refugees by their fellow Arabs with the lot of the Arabs who remained where they were, one cannot help thinking that the refugees must curse the weakness or the folly that led them to succumb to the panic propaganda of their leaders. I do not assert that Israel has done all that she could have done for the Arab minority in the 1948–67 period. I do not know the details of Israel's security problems. I take it for granted that there was excessive caution in removing the restrictions on the movements of Israeli Arabs—Israeli Jews have made the complaint frequently. But the fact remains that the Arab minority in Israel has the highest standard of living among the Arabs of the Middle East. Among the Arab representatives in Israel's Knesset (Parliament) are members of every shade of the political spectrum, including the Communist—which would be a riddle to the Communists in the jails of the Arab countries if they were permitted to know about it. The behavior of the Arab minority during the 1967 war was exemplary; not a single demonstration, not one act of sabotage; and, *per contra,* there were numerous instances of blood donations and other unforced services. I do not suggest that the Arabs of Israel would not rather live under Arab rule, but I doubt very strongly whether they would opt for it at the cost of their material condition.

Similarly, I am not in a position to deny that before 1967 Israel could safely have readmitted a larger number of refugees than she actually did. But when I think of the sustained inhumanity of the Arab states in their attitude toward their blood brothers, I simply do not understand the hue and cry raised by sentimentalists against Israel. Had half as much clamor been raised against the Arab states it is quite possible that they would have found it politically expedient to make room in the underpopulated areas of Syria and Iraq for the victims of their miscalculations.

The first, unmanageable, phase of the Arab refugee problem is behind us. In the new phase most of the refugees are on territory controlled by Israel, and that territory is, with the exception of the uninhabitable Sinai Peninsula and the tiny strip of the Golan Heights, in the truncated Palestine left after the excision of Transjordan. The likelihood that the Arab states will take any considerable number of the refugees seems as remote as ever, but now the problem is more or less manageable without them. This is one of the great gains of the 1967 victory. The uses to which this may be put will be discussed in a later chapter.

10

Sword and Trowel

(1)

ISRAEL'S War of Independence cost her close on six thousand lives. A like proportion for the United States today would be approximately two million. She gained some territory, but not enough to make her frontiers reasonably invulnerable.* She was left with the mortal narrow corridor between Jordan and the sea; she was badly exposed to incursions north, east, and south. The Suez Canal and the Gulf of 'Aqaba were closed to her in contravention of international law; her plans to develop trade connections with the Far East and the east coast of Africa were blocked.

Those rectifications that she did make in her frontiers displeased the UN, which had been impotent to protect her. The Arab states that had walked out of the court reappeared there, not to accept the original partition plan, but to charge Israel with having survived and improved her chances of survival. All they got was a hearing, which was more than they were entitled to. Israel had learned a lesson: it is good

* See map, page 5.

to have the approval of the UN, but if we make our existence conditional on it we shall not long enjoy the privilege, for we shall soon be dead.

She did not wait in 1948 for the invading armies to be thrown back before she turned to the tremendous task of the Ingathering. She began by passing a Fundamental Law that any Jew, anywhere in the world, could enter Israel and at once become a citizen. The results were staggering, and to some of us alarming. Within three years nearly a million Jews from Europe and the Arab countries—Iraq, Yemen, Syria, Egypt, Algeria, Morocco—were brought in by ship and plane. There was no accommodation for them. The houses abandoned by the Arabs could take care of only a small fraction of the number. There sprang up all over the country the hideous *maabarot,* the tent-and-tin-shack shanty towns that were the sorry best that could be done for the newcomers. Some of us believed, I among them, that the pace was unnatural. Nothing like it—the more than doubling of the population of a small, struggling country within three years—had ever been done anywhere. We believed that one hundred thousand a year would yield better results in the end. We were perhaps wrong, and now the argument is academic. What is certain is that the country went through a period of harsh austerity and of enormous, almost superhuman effort.

The temporary physical hardships that the newcomers had to endure, and those that the settled population had voluntarily assumed were not of the first importance. The pioneers of the early years had endured much more. Our anxiety was directed at the effects on the social and spiritual structure of the new state.

Since the early part of the century we had erected a highly democratic and complicated society of a unique character. Together with the private initiative sector on the land

and in the cities had grown up a network of cooperative enterprises incorporating a wide range of social principles. The famous *kibbutzim* were the most advanced. Within themselves they excluded all forms of private ownership, and in the first period some of them went so far as to communize articles of clothing, distributing them anew after every washing. Employment of outsiders for wages was forbidden as exploitation. Work was assigned, after general meetings, according to the assumed or proved ability of the individual, and living conditions were the same for all members. Much less doctrinaire was the *moshavei* (plural of *moshav*) *ovdim*, in which each family worked its own land, while the sales and purchases of the colony were conducted cooperatively. Between the *kibbutz* and the *moshav ovdim* stretched a range of compromises. The *moshavah* (to be distinguished from the *moshav*) was the classic type of privately owned farm, a stranger to the newfangled experiments.

The Histadrut, or General Federation of Labor, embraced more than three quarters of the country's workers, including those of the *kibbutzim* and the *moshavei ovdim*. It was more than a labor union. The Histadrut was, in fact, the only body of its kind in the world, for it was dedicated equally to the protection of the workers of the country, and to the bringing from abroad of as many more workers, i.e., competitors, as possible. But even without this, it was unique by virtue of a combination of features. In its other corporate capacity of *Chevrath Ovdim*, or Workers' Association, the Histadrut was the largest employer of labor in the country. Its enterprises, financed with its own funds or in partnership with private capital, included housing construction, road building, and industries of every variety. Its policies extended to the health, education, and welfare of the workers independently, as it were, of their status as workers. Its sick fund and hospitals, its press, theater, libraries, and publishing house represented the beginnings of a welfare state; this, of course, during the British administration and before the state was established.

In preparing for the termination of the mandate and the withdrawal of England, the Jewish community had built up a government within a government. The *Assefath ha-Nivharim,* or Assembly of Representatives, while lacking the coercive powers of the government itself, could bring heavy pressure to bear on groups and individuals because it had an interlocking directorate with the Histadrut. The *Vaad Leumi,* or National Council, chosen from the Assembly, was the equivalent of the Cabinet. The various governmental departments had their embryonic beginnings in the administrative units set up by the *Vaad Leumi*—finance, immigration, education, agriculture, foreign relations—these last trained as emissaries to Diaspora Jewry and to various governments.

Some of these programs were made costly by acrimonious dissensions around ideological principles. The colonies to the Left, the *kibbutzim,* were divided into two main groups—not so much, when one looked at them closely, on the issue of their structure as on the issue of their general philosophy. Some were Marxist and pro-Russian, others Socialist and anti-Russian. Some put the portrait of Karl Marx next to that of Theodor Herzl in the communal dining hall, and flew the Red flag on May 1. During the Korean War the differences within some individual settlements became so bitter than some of them split up, minority groups of moderates or extremists going over to colonies where they would join a majority. In one case a large settlement, one of the most distinguished in the country, divided on the spot.

There were long, earnest, often intemperate debates within each *kibbutz* on the methods of bringing up children, on the manner of distributing work, and, as the first period of privation passed, on the ways in which the accumulated "wealth" should be distributed. On the surface it looked as though these divisions would lead to a breakup of the *kibbutzim,* but they were actually the cementing element. The decline of the *kibbutzim,* that is—their diminished role in the upbuilding of the country—was the result of quite different causes. Not that the *kibbutzim* have ever lost their importance, but their population, increasing slowly during the great Ingathering, became a progressively smaller proportion both of the total and the agricultural population.

The history of the *kibbutzim* may be used to illustrate the danger that threatened the structure of the homeland. Among the hundreds of thousands of refugees from Europe, many had been so shattered by what they had witnessed and endured that they needed a special kind of rehabilitation. This was especially true of the young people who had spent most of their lives in surroundings that made the development of a normal attitude toward society impossible. Some were, indeed, best helped by a *kibbutz* life; the majority could not find shelter in its disciplines. The Jews who were brought in from Iraq, Yemen, Morocco, and other Arab countries had never lived under democratic governments. On the whole, they regarded governments as malevolent organisms, to be shunned or outwitted. That a government could be solicitous about their welfare was beyond their imagination. They brought with them, moreover, patriarchical mores that fought adaptation to a modern state. The equal education of sons and daughters, to take one instance, was an abomination in their eyes. Yet they had a rich culture preserved under prolonged adversity and they felt, justifiably, in no wise inferior to the Western Jews.

During the 1948–67 period the country grew at a breathless, if irregular pace; so did its problems. The differences between the Orthodox and secular sections of the community did not grow milder with the passing of time. The Orthodox, strategically placed in the political balance, imposed their religious interpretation of marriage, divorce, and inheritance on a dissenting majority. A sharp division remained, too slowly dissolving, between the Eastern and Western ethnic groups; intermarriage between them made little progress, and today amounts to less than fifteen per cent of all marriages. The Orientals, as they are called, do not share proportionately in the leadership or the upper levels of occupation and income. Much of the blame rests with the Westerners, part is due to the hangover of tradition. In elementary schools educational opportunities are the same for Orientals and Westerners, but the condition of inequality tends to perpetuate itself. The poor cannot afford to send their children to high school. The injustice bears most heavily on the women; Oriental girls are a small minority in office and secretarial employment; they are a large majority in domestic service.

The Jewish state has fallen away in other respects from the ideals and dreams of the founders. The *kibbutzim* underwent a change, diluting the purity of their socialist and egalitarian principles. To some extent the decline was forced upon them—they yielded to the national need when the floods of newcomers had to be given employment. Ben-Gurion, himself a dedicated *kibbutznik,* appealed to them to relax their Marxian orthodoxy and in the emergency sink to the level of capitalist employers. Round the *kibbutzim* sprang up settlements of recent immigrants who turned down the invitation to become *kibbutz* members, preferring to remain wage workers, free to spend their income as they liked. The *kibbutzim* thus became cooperative corporations making a profit on employees. There was also a decline in the spirit in which some of the urban cooperatives were founded. In particular, the transport cooperatives tended grossly to abuse their monopolistic position, and bus drivers became the aristocrats of labor, enjoying a far higher standard of living than other workers, higher even than that of all but the highest paid professionals.

The multiplicity of political parties inherited from the old Zionist congresses, which were a reflection of the European representative chambers, still hampers the machinery of government. Until a rational party system is created the stranglehold of the religious group on the civil life of the country will not be broken. There is still an ominous gap between export and import, and the country is still too dependent on foreign aid. Of late the rate of immigration has slowed down considerably, and the periodic depressions have not been brought under control. And there are other, larger problems facing Israel that I have yet to detail.

But when one considers against what circumstances the country has had to establish itself, one can only marvel at its essential healthiness and promise. There was a time when it looked as though the institutions so lovingly, painfully, and laboriously created by the early builders would be washed away in the flood of immigration. Everything seemed to be on the point of breaking down. A bus ride from Tel Aviv to Jerusalem was an ordeal, and hard to come by at that. One queued up for a telephone call, a postage stamp, food—what there was of it. This was the *tzena,* or austerity time, when the nation acquired a loathing for fish, then the article of diet in longest supply. It was the period of the *maabarot,* repulsive splotches on the countryside. Now the time is hardly remembered. The *maabarot* are gone, replaced by housing developments; postal and transport and telephone services are vastly improved; the fear that the political sector would dissolve into chaos has vanished. The democratic principle has endured. Israel is the only country in the Middle East where universal suffrage is unshakably rooted, where governments succeed each other by orderly election, where *coups d'état* and the suppression of political parties, however extreme to right or left, are unthinkable. There is poverty in Israel, but not hunger; the social services have been broadened; the homogenization of the population through its interpenetration by Hebrew proceeds steadily. The general level of intellectual interests is as high as the highest elsewhere.

(II)

THUS FAR I have spoken of only one set of adverse circumstances, the internal. If we go back to the beginnings and consider the external circumstances threatening the character of the Jewish settlement and the state we must wonder even more at its resistance to disintegration. The riots and massacres of 1929 struck the first blow at the ethical structure of the Zionist will: then continuously, from 1936 on, one might say that there was a conspiracy aimed at the physical and moral chances of the homeland. "We shall not let them build; and if they manage in spite of our efforts we shall see to it that nothing is left of their ideals. If we cannot rule Palestine we shall ruin it. We shall compel the little state to become a garrison, a dictatorship, a snarling, resentful organism held in contempt by the rest of the world." (One can imagine something like this in the mind of the Nazis with regard to the remnant of Jewry.)

The land has known no peace for an entire generation. From 1936 to 1939, the Arab uprising; 1939–45, the schizophrenic war; 1945–7 the rebellion against England; 1947–8, the War of Independence; and since 1948, the war on the borders, sometimes quiescent, never dead. The biblical echo from Nehemiah sounds: "They that builded the wall and they that bore burdens laded themselves, every one with one of his hands wrought in the work, and with the other held his weapon; and the builders, every one had his sword girded by his side and so builded. So we wrought in the work; and half of them held the spears from the rising of the morning till the stars appeared." A contemporary of Nehemiah, an enemy or a neutral, would have been daring indeed to predict a spiritual future of high import for the tiny state rebuilding itself under such circumstances. But out of these discouraging beginnings came the community that preserved the Bible for the world through a succession of teachers and writers, and supplied the material for Christianity and Mohammedanism. The echo speaks to the present and hints of the future.

What Israel has had to do to remain alive has not always been to her liking. The punitive, defensive actions reluctantly undertaken by the government were carried out by army units. This was a wise decision. It ran counter to the advice of shortsighted well wishers with popular views on "public relations" and "the image." It would be better, they argued, to let unidentified groups of Jews raid the offending Arab villages. But this was precisely what the government could not tolerate. It remembered the private armies of the pre-state time; it remembered the demoralization of uncontrolled retaliation; and it would not, like the Arab governments, pretend that it was unable to control its citizens.

As soon, therefore, as the raids began, the government of Israel responded openly and officially. In the years immediately following the 1948 war, the Gaza Strip was the main offender. This slice of Palestinian territory had been annexed by Egypt, and there she compelled over three hundred thousand refugees to remain in hopeless camps virtually as prisoners. She disclaimed responsibility for the *fedayeen* who crossed the border periodically to plant mines, throw bombs, and commit indiscriminate murder. And there can hardly be a doubt that in this strategy Egypt had the publicity advantage. She could not disclaim responsibility for the blockade of the Strait of Tiran or the closure of the Suez Canal to Israeli shipping and to all vessels carrying goods to and from Israel, but here again she had the advantage. The blockade established itself; it ceased to be newsworthy; but every defensive action taken by the Israeli government made the front pages.

Least of all to Israel's liking was having to make a partnership with England and France in the Sinai campaign of 1956. But it was either that or permitting the Egyptian-encouraged *fedayeen* to carry on indefinitely; and she was not strong enough to risk her existence, as she did in 1967, in single-handed combat with the Arab world.

There was naturally a great outcry against Israel's alliance with French and British imperialism, especially on the part of Egypt, who was saved on that occasion by Soviet and American imperialism. Israel also regretted that she had not taken the high risk and made the venture alone. But the outcome would have been the same. Israel would still have been forced to give up all but one of the strong positions she had captured—practically the entire Sinai Peninsula—and would still have been exposed to the danger of Arab mobilization at her very borders. What she got was the opening of the Strait of Tiran by her capture of Sharm el Sheikh; what Egypt got was a thundering scare. For nearly a decade thereafter the Gaza Strip was quiescent. In token of her willingness to refrain from doing what she dared not do, Egypt permitted the UN to station forces inside the Gaza Strip and at Sharm el Sheikh, overlooking the Strait of Tiran.

Until 1964 the raids on Israel's borders were barely tolerable; in that year they began to rise in number and quality until they called for actions that turned into miniature battles. Now it was Syria that took the main offensive and it was on the northern and eastern frontiers that the settlements lived the trowel-and-sword life. But trowel and sword are only symbols today, and the heroic builders of old were never exposed to the ingenious savageries of modern man. It filled one with horror to look up from the *kibbutzim* in the eastern Huleh Valley and on the eastern shores of the Sea of Galilee at the Golan Heights from which the Syrians, sheltered in tremendous fortifications, fired at will; it left one silent with awe and astonishment at the calm determination of the colonists. Why did they do it? Why did they cling to these perilous footholds? And how did they remain so uncorrupted in their outlook on life and their manner of thought?

Peoples and individuals must not expect preferential treatment, and only in very exceptional cases may they plead the world's wickedness as a complete excuse for their own. But though the case of Jewry and of Israel is exceptional, such a plea does not have to be made. Their performance would have been credible in a much kinder world; in the world as it is they merit, if not preferential treatment, at least a high rating on the list of today's civilizing centers.

11

The Dark Hours

FOR those to whom Israel was an intimate possession —and we were many more than we suspected—the last weeks in May and the first week in June 1967 were a nightmare. The dread of the unpredictable was intensified, as it is in certain nightmares, by a foreboding of calamity deepening against the illusory presence of the means of rescue. The threat of destruction grew inexorably from day to day: the precipitous withdrawal of the United Nations force from the Gaza Strip, the blockade of the Strait of Tiran, the mobilization of the Egyptian, Jordanian, and Syrian armies on the frontiers of Israel. The possibility of rescue, known to be illusory but refusing to be dismissed, hovered over the mock-meaningful debates in the UN, the intrigues, maneuvers, and contrived delays. One thought of a quaint and macabre pavane conducted in the senate by the elders of a city within sound of approaching barbarian hordes. Behind the UN the maritime powers footled with the idea of a challenge to the blockade while soothing counsels of patience poured upon Israel together with expressions of regard that sounded increasingly like the prelude to a regretful and generous obituary.

The gathering protest that went up from the liberal world had a curious double effect. It heartened us in the feeling of the rightness of our cause; it depressed us with the question we would not ask: "Where were you till now?"

Israel was quiet; there was neither panic nor the will to war; there was intensifying impatience, but no public demonstration—all of which was misinterpreted by the Arab heads of state, who were convinced that Israel would not fight, she would rather die of slow asphyxiation than face the combined Arab armies; and that if she did fight she would be annihilated. Nasser would have preferred the first alternative; however, he did not mind the second.

We were told later that American military intelligence had foreseen Israel's lightning victory. If Israel had not destroyed the Arab air force on the ground in the first hour of the war, she would have destroyed it in the air in the first two or three days. The record of earlier clashes between the Israeli and Arab air forces supports this view, but what would have happened in those two or three days, with Tel Aviv, Haifa, Jerusalem within a few minutes' flight from the Arab airfields? Israel prepared a hundred thousand beds for civilian casualties; Egypt prepared none, confident that the Israelis would not bomb cities.

The nightmare touched bottom on the morning of June 5 and stayed weltering there for perhaps two days, for we did not dare to trust at once the marvelous good news that reached us. An initial Arab victory, or at least an invasion of Israel, seemed a possibility, though the talk of "annihilating Israel," "sweeping Israel into the sea," "bringing back the refugees to take possession" was, for those of us who knew the land and the people well, nothing more than lunatic babbling. We knew that the physical destruction of Israel was an enterprise beyond the power of the Arab states. It would call for the removal or slaughter of over two million Jews. Removal whither? Let us make the highly improbable assumption that within ten years of an Arab invasion of Israel a number of countries would have consented to receive a total of half a million refugees (I leave to the imagination of the reader the appeals, the conferences, the debates that would precede any substantial action). What of those ten years? What of the years following?

Can Arab leaders have believed in the promise they were making to the deluded Arab masses? Can those that are still repeating it believe in it now? If the example of Nazi Germany beckoned to them, their case was indeed hopeless. What would have taken place in Israel would not have been a "cleaning out," a *Gleichschaltung,* but the rise of a resistance movement of unexampled ferocity and endurance. The fury of the Warsaw Ghetto uprising would have infected every man, woman, and child in Israel, but instead of forty thousand hollow-eyed, disease-ridden unarmed survivors of years of debilitating torment, there would have faced the Arabs a people of two million, armed to the teeth, supported and encouraged by an outraged world Jewry and by democratic opinion in every free country, and not without a large body of sympathizers in Communist countries.

But we need not confine ourselves to the past tense. The same dread spectacle should haunt those Arab leaders who still dream or at least talk of a military victory over Israel, the more dread since Israel's fighting will has been so grimly reconfirmed. The controlled defensive raids carried out by the Israelis in the past against Jordan and Syria would be child's play compared with the outbursts of murder and sabotage that would rage within the country and beyond its borders. All the energies, resourcefulness, devotion, and determination that have gone into the creation of the Jewish state would be channeled into the furious protest of a people at bay. The terrorists of the closing years of the British occupation would return a hundredfold. Bands would take to the hills and roam the countryside, cutting off communications, blowing up installations, paralyzing agriculture and industry. It would be insensate to think of sending hundreds of thousands of Arabs to occupy such a land, let alone govern it. The area would be turned into a plague spot for generations to come.

In that sense, and in that sense alone, Israel could be destroyed. The schools, the universities, the institutes of science, the elaborate structure of democratic government and social responsiblilty would go, together with Israel's participation in the development of backward nations. For whose benefit? Not for that of the Arab peoples, nor for that of their backers, and least of all for that of the Arab refugees.

These were the black thoughts that haunted us, alternating with others scarcely less oppressive. The Arab leaders did not talk terms, although they pretended to. When they demanded, *pro forma,* nothing more than Israel's return to the borders drawn by the United Nations in 1947, they did not conceal their larger plans. Even if they had taken the trouble to do so, one would have had to be dim-witted indeed to believe that after a victory in 1967 they would be content with what they had contemptuously rejected after defeat in 1948. Exploring the second black alternative, we asked ourselves: suppose that after a long bloodletting a defeated Israel accepts the crazy frontiers of 1947, or even those of 1948; and suppose that the Arabs, weakened in the struggle, respect them for a number of years—the best we could hope for—what then? What a double load of preparation we would have to carry for the next war! As it is, a huge slice of Israel's budget has been absorbed by defense needs, and apart from the monetary waste there has been a dreadful waste of energies, inventiveness, and emotions. It would be beyond human capacity to go on living, working, creating, nurturing a dream under the new circumstances and in the certainty that another war was coming; for in the Arab mind there is no place for the idea of a limited victory.

When the miracle happened it was, as the word implies, as if the ordinary course of nature had been suspended. For the moment the world was bathed in an unnatural light shining on Israel. The immense feeling of gratitude and relief was suffused with incredulity. And when the details came through, and the manner of the victory was explained, the sense of the miraculous was increased, not diminished. It was doubly miraculous that all this should have happened without a suspension of the ordinary course of nature.

The preparation and training over the years had been thorough, the planning perfect. But where there is a will, preparation may be expected; and a plan is only as good as its execution, which depends on the quality of the arms. Israel's citizen army has been called the best in the world for its size. What made it so?

We are accustomed to thinking of an army's efficiency in terms of tradition, particularly as incorporated in an officer corps. West Point, Sandhurst, St. Cyr, Berlin are associated with generations of soldiers; they are the breeding places of a particular species of men, the planners and leaders on the battlefield. The common soldier may have every incentive to fight, he may be fearless and hardy, and even without a first class officer corps he may acquit himself well, but in the organized collision of a set battle he is lost.

There is no Israeli West Point or Sandhurst or St. Cyr. There are of course professional soldiers, but there is no soldierly tradition. There are no traditions of *l'honneur* and *la gloire*; even the phrase "an officer and a gentleman" is not translatable into Hebrew, much less into Yiddish.

It is not enough to repeat, as it has often been done, that the Israelis had no alternative but to win. The knowledge that there was no retreat but into the sea—together with wife, children, brothers, sisters, parents—accounts for the resoluteness of the Israeli soldier; it does not account for his skill, his daring, and his initiative; nor does it account for the matchless performance of the military machine.

We have learned that the Israeli officer in the field never issues the command "Forward!" but always "Follow me!" We have also learned that in the casualty lists of the Israeli army the proportion of officers runs as high as twenty-five to thirty per cent, unheard of elsewhere. The Israeli officer is extraordinarily attentive to the welfare of his men and every life is to him a precious thing. These are some of the features of a good fighting machine. If you add them to all the others that distinguish the Israeli army and look for the source of the total, you will find it in the sum of Jewish history. In Egypt, in the presence of the Pyramids, Napoleon made his famous address to the army: ". . . forty centuries look down upon you . . ." In the Israeli citizen army forty centuries were alive.

One would have said, sixty years ago, that the most difficult transformation the Jews would have to undergo in Palestine would be in the military field. The earliest of the neo-Zionist colonies were founded in the 1880's and 1890's. In a land where banditry and thievery were common, every colony had its own guards, but the Jewish colonies employed Arab guards, who were not noted for their trustworthiness. It was not until 1906 that the first group of *shomrim,* Jewish guards, was formed, and they obtained employment from the old colonists with great difficulty. Out of the *shomrim* was to grow, indirectly, the Jewish self-defense of the mandate period, and out of the Haganah has grown Israel's army. As individual fighters the Jews had established their reputation long before 1948, but as organizers of a modern army their reputation began with the War of Independence, and was partly confirmed in the Sinai campaign. But in 1948 the fighting was still half of the guerrilla type, and in 1956 the participation of the English and French obscured to some extent the achievement of the Israelis. Only in this last war has Israel leapt to an unchallengeable place in the front rank of the militarily proficient nations.

In all their other transformations, from city dwellers to dwellers in open places, from inhabitants of the Temperate Zone into inhabitants of a subtropical zone, from merchants and white-collar workers into farmers and industrialists, the Jews were helped over obstacles by conscious and formulated ideals. They *wanted* to leave the cities, they *wanted* to become farmers and workers, and so they bore with the hardships of a subtropical climate. But they did *not* want to become fighters. *Jews do not like fighting.* The joy of battle is as alien to them as alcoholism. Delight in battle with their peers is a doubly offensive suggestion. This lack of inclination is very old and goes back to the Bible, where the only cry of exultation in battle comes from the horse in Job, "who sayeth ha! ha! among the trumpets." There is fighting enough in the biblical annals, and of the bloodiest kind, but though there is exultation in victory, nowhere is war as such exalted in song, or justified in philosophy as "the father of all things." The experience of the Exile deepened the Jewish abhorrence of physical combat, and in process of time the spectacle of one empire after another failing to perpetuate itself by war vindicated the philosophy interwoven with the abhorrence.

There was not much exultation in the victory of 1967. Except for a moment of delirium before the Western Wall there were no victory demonstrations, and that was really a moment of passionate reunion. I have been told of a press correspondent who was asked to send back to America reports of dancing in the streets and had to cable back that there hadn't been any.

Joy in deliverance was overshadowed by the thought of the dead. What moved the nation more than anything else was the tremendous pulse of unification. Suddenly all political, ethnic, and social differentiations disappeared. "Westerner" and "Oriental," rightist and leftist, worker, executive, employer, *sabra,* and recent arrival forgot their quarrels and grievances. After the victory there was no squabbling for a share in the credit, no recriminations, no part of the population was accused of having given less than its best. The old differences will reappear, of course, and with them vast new problems. But on every hand I heard, "It will never be the same again. We really didn't know our own feelings."

Those feelings must be understood as practical realities; they constitute Israel's peculiar historical morale. Arab writers are fond of harking back to the Crusaders as an example of intruders who managed to establish themselves in the country for a while, only to be driven out when the inevitable moment came. The analogy will not stand a moment's scrutiny. The Crusaders came as conquistadors to carve out kingdoms and collect booty. They were certainly intruders, with no historic roots in the territory. They did not feel a homecoming, did not settle down to till the soil of their ancestors and resume a long-frustrated national destiny. Their life's business was elsewhere.

As the Israelis had not known their own feelings, so they had not known how deeply world Jewry felt with them. They had been skeptical of Zionist sentiment among the Jews in the affluent West. They asked, "Why aren't you here in larger numbers? You give sympathy, money, political influence; you do not give yourselves." The question is still asked, but not as impatiently or scornfully. The response of Diaspora Jewry was too massive to be accepted with a shrug, and the sense of unity flowed out far beyond the borders of Israel. Israel now knew—and this was one of the deep sources of satisfaction—that Diaspora Jewry was tied to it by bonds of greater strength than either had realized. If Western Jewries have sent only token numbers of settlers the reason is not simply the addiction to a comfortable life. That is only one element among others of a larger meaning.

I have spoken of what world Jewry and Israel owe to America. The Bible confers upon Cyrus the Persian, who made possible the Return after the First Destruction, the title of messiah, or anointed. America has played a messianic role in the second Return. The American Jew has two loves: America and Israel. I will not say he is torn between them; they are connected in a single vision for mankind. If it were only the memory of what he escaped from when America for a time held wide open her gates, the Jew must think of America with love and gratitude; but there was more than escape. In America, Jewish life found an efflorescence unique in the history of the Diaspora. America's destiny, her struggles with herself, her successes and failures and perplexities, have engaged the Jew with a special intimacy. He would leave America with regret, consoled only by the knowledge that he is not relinquishing her ideals.

Something of this has come through to Israel, mitigating the sharpness of the question. Of greater consequence is the dawning recognition that world Jewry is not headed for early assimilation. It has a long life before it and must make provision accordingly. Its greatest asset is its unity with Israel, and this same unity is Israel's greatest asset on the world scene. Not only is it impossible, it is not desirable that the Diaspora shall be absorbed into Israel. Both must remain as the two wings of a world people. In the light that followed the dark hours of 1967 this truth was made to stand out with a new clarity.

12

Russia and Jewry

A STANDARD form of posthumous political comment runs: "Russia (England, America) would have done better to . . ." Such comment has merit only if it takes into account that nations and individuals do what they do because of what they have done before. Russia would certainly have done better to tell Egypt and Syria in 1964 not to start pushing Israel to the wall; she would then have been spared the resounding slap in the face she got in 1967. Unfortunately such a warning did not suit Russia in 1964, although what has happened since suits her even less.

One might go further back and say: "Russia would have done better to follow up her original action in voting (and with such warmth!) for a Jewish state by promoting friendship and understanding between Israel and her neighbors." Quite true; and this would have been all the easier, it would seem, in the light of Russia's not unfriendly attitude toward Israel until 1955. There was, of course, the matter of Russia's anti-Semitism, which has to be considered at some length. But it is quite conceivable that Russia could have indulged her anti-Semitism at home while promoting a

Jewish state in a confederation of Arab states, just as Egypt jails Communists while cooperating with Russia internationally. Russia had only to make a distinction between Israelis and Jews or, as it is usually put, between the right kind of Jews and the wrong kind. It would admittedly have been the same difficult job to reconcile the Arabs to the existence of a Jewish state, but now it has to be done anyhow, and Russia is much worse off than if she had started twenty years ago.

Unfortunately, again, for these helpful comments, the old Russian ambition to dominate the Middle East and the eastern Mediterranean, which gave England and France so much trouble in the nineteenth century, saw a new chance when Nasser came to power and proclaimed a socialist future for his country and for the Arab world. That Israel was more socialist than the Arab world was likely to become for a century or more was of no consequence, and Russia began the adventure that culminated in the 1967 debacle. One would have to go very far back to set Russia on a sensible course.

A belated lesson can also be read to Israel from the other side. She would have done better to turn Communist, take in fewer refugees, and cut her ties with world Jewry. She would now be—perhaps—one of the "freedom-loving peoples fighting against neo-colonialism." And she would not be encouraging Jews to feel more Jewish everywhere in the world, including Russia.

This may, in fact, be her greatest offense. Russia wants to get rid of her Jews. That is to say, she wants them to forget their Jewish identity, and she is applying to that end all means short of physical violence. Under Stalin physical violence rose to a pitch of mass murder. Jewish writers and intellectuals were liquidated or sent to perish in Siberia. Today the means are more subtle, but the objective is the same and the effect as cruel. I do not intend to marshal the evidence here; it is obtainable elsewhere in such overwhelming detail that those who dismiss it can do so only because they approve of Russia's policy.

All that I wish to do here is to describe the character of Russian anti-Semitism. It descends in a straight line from the anti-Semitism of the Czarist period, sharing with it a detestation of the Jewish people. But while the Czarist government used enforced emigration as one method of getting rid of the Jews, Communist Russia has shut the doors from within and uses enforced assimilation on its captives. In the Czarist era a Jew could free himself of all legal disabilities—the *numerus clausus* in the high schools and universities, residential restrictions, travel handicaps, exclusion from officer rank in the army, etc.—by the simple act of baptism. It did not have to be the Greek Orthodox Church; Catholicism would do, or a branch of Protestantism, as long as it meant repudiation of the Jewish religion. But since in Communist Russia the repudiation of religion is the universal prerequisite for a career, the Jew cannot distinguish himself by becoming an atheist. He must surrender what no one else is asked to surrender—his ethnic identity. Such a surrender was not demanded by Czarist Russia. Jews could and did register as Christian by faith and Jewish by nationality.

For the Jew a change of ethnic identity is somewhat more complicated than a baptism. It calls for a relinquishment of Jewish associations; it calls for a suppression of a special curiosity about Jews and the Jewish community; above all, it calls for a cancellation of any ties one may feel with Jews in other countries.

There are still strong survivals of Jewish cultural and traditional attachments among Russian Jews. They are granted niggardly indulgence in order to avoid the scandal of a too obvious repression. A Yiddish monthly is published in Kiev, and once or twice a year a Yiddish anthology is published, occasional Jewish concerts and plays are organized;

but the satisfaction of Jewish interests in the medium of Russian is forbidden. No books or periodicals in the local language, such as are abundant wherever Jewish communities are found in democratic countries, devoted to Jewish culture, history, current events, or contemporaneous problems, are permitted. One must satisfy one's interests in Yiddish or not at all. Hebrew does not even come into the question. But since in Russia, as in America, the majority of Jews know neither Hebrew nor Yiddish, they are simply cut off from the only possible channel of communication and counsel with their fellow Jews. It need hardly be said that whatever reports they get in the official press (including the Yiddish monthly) about Jews in other countries are even more distorted than reports about matters in general abroad. The reports on Israel, which I touch on below, are of a special character.

The official policy of equality for de-Judaized Jews has been carried out in some areas, with allowance for local or individual anti-Semitisms and the effect of the government attitude toward the Jewish religion. In the sciences the Jews are well represented; they contribute more than their numerical share of physicists and mathematicians, though it is a question whether this share corresponds to their share of talent. In the diplomatic service they are hardly represented at all, in government far less than they were in the Stalin-Trotzky period. On the whole, it may be said that Jews who have lost or abandoned their associations with their people can get by.

The government's attitude toward religion vitiates whatever sincerity there is in its acceptance of the completely de-Judaized Jew. The attacks on the Jewish religion that pass the censorship are unlike the attacks on other religions. They are of such a scurrilous and indecent character that in some cases Communists in the Western countries have voiced their protest, and one of the offending publications was withdrawn, although as far as is known the writers have never been called to task. The text in these publications is accompanied by illustrations in which the faces and postures of the religious Jews might have been or actually were copied from the most noxious Czarist and Nazi gutter sheets: the same hooked bird-of-prey noses, thick slobbering lips, and deformed hyena-like bodies. The publishers of these books and pamphlets will no doubt argue that only religious Jews have such repulsive physical characteristics; the idea will not occur to the simple reader.

Among the Jewish members of the Communist Party will be found some who lend their names to publications of this kind. To them the Jewish religion is hateful in a peculiar, personal way, and they have helped to set the tone of the government toward Judaism. Out of the badly remembered religious Jewish education of their childhood they have supplied the scraps of misinformation, the fragmentary quotations that lend an "inside" touch to a book like *Judaism Without Embellishment.* (The same device was used in Czarist days.) Their rancor is that of an assimilating Jew who is convinced that his advancement among Gentiles has been blocked by the detestable Jewishness of other Jews; and perhaps the *Yevsektzia,* the now dissolved Jewish branch of the Communist Party, had reason to feel that way when the ax descended on it not less bloodily than on unde-Judaizing Jews. *Yevsektzia* members and their survivors are more anxious than non-Jewish anti-Semites that the Jewish religion shall be more harshly treated than other religions, that the supplies of ritual objects and prayer-books accorded it shall fall below the level for the other religions, that a Jewish religious seminary shall not be opened, and that the Jewish religion shall not be treated with the same indulgence as in other Communist countries, such as Romania, for instance, which even permits a national federation of rabbis.

A peculiarly nasty twist is imparted to Soviet anti-Semitism by the theoretical status of the Jew in Russia. According to the basic law the Jews constitute a nationality, like the Ukranians, the Germans, the Uzbeks, and so on. Every Jew, like every other Russian subject, carries an "internal" passport, or identity card. If both his parents are Jewish, the word Jewish (*Yevrei,* Hebrew) is stamped on the passport, whether he wants it or not. If only one of his parents is Jewish, he has the option of adopting the nationality of his non-Jewish parent. A Jew intent on sloughing or concealing his Jewish identity must curse the endogamous perversity of his parents; but he may console himself with the thought that he at least will not pass the affliction on to his children.

The rights or privileges of the nationalities within the Soviet Union are clearly set forth in the constitution. They are entitled to schools in their own languages, and where they happen to have a tiny enclave within another nationality they are even entitled to separate classes in their own languages on the request of a dozen families. They have their own newspapers, higher institutes of learning, courts, and theaters. Since the government controls all supplies, this means that voluntary associations cannot by themselves exercise, as in other countries, their cultural freedom; they must get the supplies, printing plants, paper, buildings, etc., from the government. In the Jewish case the request for schools, periodicals, theaters, etc., comes from a minority within a minority. But a minority within a minority, though it may number several hundred thousand, is at a disadvantage, especially in Russia. The Soviet government offers the argument that the majority don't want these facilities; whence it would appear that it is undemocratic on the part of the minority to want them. One must not be undemocratic in Russia. As for those Jews by nationality who still have some bonds with their people but know only Russian

—and their number, indeterminate, is certainly a large one —they simply have no exercisable Jewish rights.

If the Jews and their religion have been singled out in this fashion for discrimination or opprobrium, part of the reason, as I have indicated, is to be found in Czarist tradition. Anti-Semitism was a general feature of the ruling class. But anti-Semitism was and is also useful as a political instrument. Czarist officialdom raged at the Jew for being a revolutionary, on the one hand, and a capitalist exploiter, especially of the peasantry, on the other. Communist Russia has denounced the Jew as a black marketeer on the one hand and a rootless cosmopolitan on the other. Whatever malignant forces have been made the explanation of some particular difficulty in Russian life, they have been discovered as emanating from the Jew.

Another important aspect of Soviet anti-Semitism is related to the political complexion of Western Jewry as it has developed since the emancipation in the early part of the nineteenth century. This has been predominantly liberal. Only a small though prominent section belonged to the revolutionary left, and a somewhat larger section to the reactionary right. The main body was liberal and progressive on ethical as well as political grounds. Marx and Lassalle represent the revolutionary left; Heine, Börne, Moses Hess were what we would call today liberals (in their day they were counted as revolutionaries). Now, it is a significant fact that the affirmation of Jewish identity was very strong in the last three. Heine and Börne were both concerned in their early years with the preservation of Judaism. Heine's baptism, which he often regretted and despised, did not put an end to his inner association with the Jewish people, which haunted him until the end. Hess began as an extreme revolutionary and as the associate of Karl Marx; in his middle life he reverted with the passion of a convert to Jewish nationalism, being in fact the earliest of the political

Zionists. His booklet *Rome and Jerusalem,* advocating a Jewish state in Palestine, preceded Herzl's *Judenstaat* by more than thirty years.

The progressivism of the Western Jew made him a natural enemy of the revolutionary, and he was much more dangerous than the reactionary, for like all progressives he was undercutting the revolutionary program, while the reactionary by his rigidity was giving it greater appeal. In the reactionary the revolutionary sees his open enemy, while the progressive, who pretends to seek the same ends as the revolutionary by peaceful means, is the hypocritical and more dangerous enemy. And as long as Russia makes a pretense of favoring world revolution, she must prefer reactionary to liberal governments: assuming of course that the reactionary governments are not, as Germany was, powerful enough to threaten her safety.

Thus Russia would prefer a reactionary to a progressive Israel. It would make her case more convincing. She can and does make the world ring with her denunciations of Israel as a fascist or Nazi tool of Western imperialism, but she finds the going hard—witness the sympathy Israel has won for herself in liberal and even leftist circles. Her reports on the war of 1967 were received with contempt in the Western world, where a free press gave it, during and after those six days, tremendous coverage, with continuous radio and TV accompaniment. I pick at random a little "eyewitness" sketch supplied by the correspondent of the *Komsomolskaya Pravda* (circulation 7 million):

> The Israelis celebrated the taking of Jerusalem for several days. The slightly tight officers jumped to the sound of *"freilich"* in the abandoned taverns. *"Atem be-Israel toda la-el,"* [You are in Israel, thank God], Don't be afraid. Let us make merry together," they assured the girls they saw by chance. And at the same time, near the Gates of Purification, having

tied up their police dogs, soldiers roared with laughter and rolled their eyes, looking at their girl friends in military uniform jumping rope. . . .

This must be given top marks for comical clumsiness. The one weakness Jews and Israelis are known not to be addicted to is liquor, and those who remember the scenes of religious fervor when soldiers and civilians rushed headlong to the Western Wall must turn from this description in disgust. But though it got through to the West, this exquisite sample of Russian reportage was meant for home consumption. Even as such it may not have been very effective. Judging from the Yiddish and Hebrew words it was written by a Jew who cannot have been ignorant of his people's habits; one gets the impression that he does not quite believe his own words.

The same may be said of Russian anti-Israel propaganda in general. The drummers lack their onetime vim and the drums themselves have gone somewhat flaccid. The viciousness is still there, but the drive is absent. Russia's new line, since she took over the Arab cause and began supplying Egypt and Syria with arms while suddenly branding Israel as the spearhead of neocolonialism in the Middle East, has had a weak market in the Communist world.

One reason is that it goes against the grain of elementary human sentiment. The sight of a small group standing up resolutely to an immensely superior enemy must evoke instinctive sympathy where heart and mind are not wholly warped. Communists are apt to get angry when they hear the cliché, "You can't change human nature." I hope they will be lenient with this particular manifestation of it; there is comfort in the thought that whatever other bourgeois prejudices must go, this one will remain.

Perhaps they will grant the point, but add, "Suppose the little resolute group consisted of a band of fanatical Nazis holding out against the world, what would you say then?" And this returns us to the political game and Russia's need to blacken Israel's character, particularly with the Nazi smear.

With her belated discovery that Israel is a tool of Western imperialism, Russia has created a vast and unmanageable setting for the problems facing Israel and her neighbors. Now a regional settlement cannot be tolerated because of its repercussions two thousand miles away. Israel's war of self-defense must be represented as a dark plot against Arab self-liberation. A summary of this view is given by the monthly *Sovietsky Soyuz* (*Soviet Union*) of July 1967:

> Already in May the American and British press, radio, and television began an intensive working over of world public opinion in order to represent in advance the action of the Israel invaders as the "defense" of their right to "existence." This stand of the western powers is not accidental. The memory of the Suez adventure of 1956 is still fresh. What happened now was a clear attempt to revenge. It has undoubtedly been hastened by the clear wish of the interested imperialist circles to liquidate the progressive regimes in the UAR, Syria, and Algeria, to deliver a blow against the anti-imperialist movement of the Arabs and to restore the colonial order in the Near East. . . . The smell of petroleum emanates from all the arms delivered to Israel from abroad.

Russian arms delivered to the Middle East must, with the postwar panicky additions, surpass all other deliveries combined. In Russian nostrils they are odorless; to Jewish nostrils they bring a whiff of Czarism and pogroms.

13

The Humiliation of the Arabs

"It was a mistake," the Russians told the Arabs soon after the war, "to have kept on proclaiming your intention to destroy Israel." It was a greater mistake on Russia's part not to have told this to the Arabs years before. But it was apparently the proclamation, not the intention, that was the error. It was bad publicity, and it sharpened the fighting edge of the Israelis. Now the Arabs too are saying that they never intended to destroy Israel. It was just talk, and Israel, with memories of Hitler, overreacted.

Why didn't the Russians offer their sage advice to the Arabs before? Obviously, because it would not have been taken; also, perhaps, because the Russians, who are better double-thinkers than the Arabs, may have thought that the propaganda could be switched on and off among the Arabs as abruptly as among the Russians. In any case, the Arab leaders could not have whipped up hatred of Israel without promising Israel's destruction. They could not have abused the condition of the Arab refugees for nineteen years in order to acquiesce willingly in the fact of Israel's existence. The refugees would not have endured such treatment without the promise that they were going to re-enter a Palestine cleansed of the Jewish state; and that, by the 1960's, meant cleansed of the Jews.

The 300,000 refugees in the Gaza Strip, living mostly in camps, were not permitted to enter Egypt, of which the Gaza Strip was now a part, and look for work there. The 300,000 in Lebanon and Syria were in somewhat better case. They could move around. In Syria some of them were given employment. Little Kuwait, the richest per capita country in the world, gave employment to between 60,000 and 80,000. But neither in these countries nor in Iraq were the refugees permitted to become citizens, and it must be borne in mind that Syria and Iraq are underpopulated. Lebanon had her own problem; the refugees were nearly all Moslems, and in Lebanon a delicate balance must be maintained between the Christian and Moslem populations.

Jordan alone offered the refugees both employment and citizenship, but her means were limited; and even Jordan, while offering citizenship, paradoxically followed the practice of the other Arab countries in insisting that the refugee retain the status of refugee; he was so identified; whether he wanted it or not, he was to consider that his proper place was where he had been before 1948—he was not to think of settling permanently anywhere else.

The condition of the refugees varied considerably, but for the great majority, particularly in the Gaza Strip, it was miserable in the extreme. UNRWA (United Nations Relief and Works Agency for Palestine Refugees) met three of their basic needs—rations, medical aid, and education (not all three everywhere)—and nearly seventy per cent of the bill was footed by the United States. The education in the UNRWA schools was laced, as elsewhere, with violent anti-Israel propaganda, and a generation grew up infected from childhood with hatred of Israel. It was a generation that had not known a normal life, and the one hope that was held out to it was the reconquest of Palestine and the ejection of the Jews.

The refugees had become a valuable political property, not to be dissipated on humanitarian grounds. There was a common concern for its perpetuation, and behind that, fierce rivalries in its exploitation. Remote Algeria sought to snatch the leadership of the Arab world from Egypt; so did Syria, whose relations with Egypt were envenomed by a brief, unsuccessful marriage. Iraq, Saudi Arabia, and the small oil El Dorados dreaded Egypt's domination, but Nasser had established a tremendous hold on the imagination of Arabs everywhere. Thus far, the crushing military defeat of 1967 has not broken it. Nasser has been the master exploiter of the refugees, in whose humiliation all the other Arab states have concurred.

They also concurred with him in his anti-Westernism. But this is a beclouded issue. The Arabs want the benefit of Western technology, and also want the West to keep its nose out of their affairs—two desiderata not easily reconciled. Nasser plays skillfully on the xenophobia of the Arab masses: at the same time he must invite German and Russian technicians into Egypt. The oil-rich countries have had to submit to the development of their resources by American, British, and Italian experts and capitalists; the rulers resent the price they have had to pay, and to that extent they are wholly with Nasser's anti-Westernism. But the xenophobia upon which Nasser plays inspires the masses with a feeling of strength and the rulers with uneasiness. It is perhaps more dangerous for them than Nasser's direct invasion through Yemen. An even greater danger would have been a victory over Israel, which would have made Nasser an irresistible force among the Arab masses. It was with relief as well as out of fear that the oil-rich Arab countries made Nasser a grant of over a quarter of a billion dollars to help him over the consequences of his defeat.

Nasser's political strategy has been described as Bismarckian—an appeal over the heads of petty rulers for national unity. Some resemblance is there, but it is weak by comparison with another feature: the creation of a national mob spirit through foreign adventure in order to carry through reforms at home. Nasser has earned his reputation as a progressive by his program of nationalization, but to carry it through he has had to debauch the public spirit of the country to a degree not exceeded by communism and Nazism at their worst. It is not enough to say that the Egyptian masses are kept in ignorance of fateful facts, that not a questioning whisper is permitted, that a hint of opposition is suicidal. Egypt has been turned into a lunatic asylum among whose inmates delusions are propagated by an unchallenged head keeper. And what is most frightening is that an echo of the delusions is heard in the outside world.

Amid the general admiration and astonishment at Israel's victory, voices were raised in as strange a protest as has ever been recorded. The victory was too complete! It was a humiliation of the Arabs! It was not Nasser who had humiliated the Arabs, it was the Israelis. And in order to restore the self-respect of the Arabs the Israelis ought to do something for Nasser and the other Arab leaders.

But what the Israelis were really being asked to do was to add to the humiliation of the Arabs by confirming Nasser in his leadership. How it was to be done was never made clear. Were the Israelis to offer some kind of apology for having defended their lives with such lethal efficiency? Ought they to have pretended that they won by accident, leaving the Arabs with the heartening impression that the next time the outcome might be different?

The Arab refugees had been humiliated for nineteen years by their fellow Arabs, but not these were asked to make amends. The Arab masses had been humiliated by Nasser, who had played with them, lied to them, poisoned them into an insanity of blood lust, but it was not he who was asked to make amends. That role was assigned to Israel, the people and the state he had set out to destroy. I find it difficult to listen to this kind of talk. As there is nothing more tedious than the complaints of an unsuccessful scoundrel, so there is nothing sillier than sob-sister compassion over his downfall.

Much, perhaps too much, has been written about the Arabs' power of self-delusion, their unique addiction to living in the realm of fantasy, their intoxication with words. These are not inborn aptitudes; they are acquired or implanted and can be eradicated. They explain why there is no grass-roots political life in the Arab countries, and therefore why it is so difficult to come to an understanding with the Arabs. The leaders have so completely compromised themselves on the issue of the destruction of Israel that some time must pass before sufficient numbers can reverse themselves to risk a bid for power. Revolt from below is a long way off.

Anyone who saw on television the Cairo mobs howling for war and the blood of Israel must feel discouraged. They horrified more than they frightened; their nightmarish bloodthirstiness suggested hysteria; they did not give the impression of strength; they were in fact pitiable as well as sickening. But they horrified because they were playacting out the suggestions of their leader; they were without resistance, without a foothold. It would have been reassuring to infer that the armies concentrated in the Sinai were as empty of inner strength. But how could one tell? This was the rabble, not the trained army with its hundreds of planes and tanks, its other modern equipment—and Israel's cities within a few minutes of the Egyptian airfields.

To absolve a man of all moral responsibility is to tell him to go to hell, for it is to take away from him all hope of rehabilitation. Unless I am wholly wrong in my views, the

Arab mobs were guilty in yielding to Nasser's manipulations. Their sufferings in defeat will teach them nothing if they are encouraged to believe that Nasser was right and they therefore right in obeying him.

Very depressing is the absence, even in exile, of an Arab intellectual elite with an independent point of view. Even if Nasser were right this would be a bad sign; as it is, it cannot be worse. A few days before the war broke out Jean-Paul Sartre issued a 992-page number of his periodical *Les Temps modernes,* on which he and his colleagues had been working for two years. It was an attempt to get the Jewish and Arab intellectuals together at least on paper. He succeeded after a fashion. "All that these pages contain," he says in a prefatory note, "is the inert coexistence of two collections of information." But what a difference between the two collections!

The Israeli intellectuals wrote freely, with criticisms of their government, with occasional suggestions at complete variance with the Zionist purpose. The non-Israeli Arab intellectuals spoke with one uncritical voice. More than that, they threatened in a body to withdraw their articles if a contribution was accepted from the Algerian Razak Abdel-Kader, a partisan of Arab-Jewish reconciliation.

The lock-step uniformity of outlook in the seventeen non-Israeli Arabs would be distressing enough if the intellectual level were acceptable. It is wretchedly low. All the old standard terminology of the Left is mechanically, indiscriminately applied, with about as much relevance to contemporaneous conditions as the phlogiston theory has to modern chemistry. But for these Arab writers it seems to be *le dernier cri* in political philosophy. Apart from this, the essays reflect an astonishing ignorance of history. They are mentioned only because they are a part of the melancholy picture of Arab helplessness.

14

Prisoners of Yesterday

FINDING the incident that triggered the Israeli-Arab war of 1967 would be about as useful as identifying the chamois whose hoofbeat precipitated an Alpine avalanche. We must try instead to determine what caused the accumulation of forces that exploded on June 5. And we must begin by throwing off the shackles of terminologies and concepts belonging to the world of yesterday.

There is a struggle between communism and capitalism, but it has nothing to do with the "colonialism" and "imperialism" and "exploitation" which are the staples of current Communist propaganda. Whatever economic value colonies once had, they have none today; colonialism is dead, and what is called "neocolonialism" has no connection with the purposes colonialism once had; "imperialism" means something it has never meant before, and the use of the word is misleading. Domination of small countries by great powers does not, with some fading exceptions, aim primarily at economic gain.

The rivalry between Communist and non-Communist powers (for the sake of brevity, I shall speak of Russia and

America, leaving out the complication of China) is one of the most curious phenomena in history. On the surface it seems to bespeak a pure idealism. Each side is prepared to pay heavily, also to take part in costly wars, in order to bring the benefits of its own system to faraway countries. As an investment, the transaction is an absurdity, and is known to be so. What then is the incentive? It is the hope of seeing a given area develop the economic system of one of the two rivals, the hope of seeing as much of the world as possible under the sign of communism or capitalism.

This, too, will before long become an absurdity. America and Russia are converging toward an approximate similarity of form. As America improves in the distribution of wealth and the management of the Negro problem, as Russia moves out of her Czarist-induced dictatorship form of society and her Czarist inheritance of anti-Semitism, as liberalism spreads in America and emerges in Russia, as American corporation capitalism and Russia state capitalism are brought under more effective popular control, the two powers will be waging more and more of a Homoousion-Homoiousion war. But "before long"—which may mean as much as fifty years—is still important today. Shall the newly-developing areas pass into the hoped-for better future via primitive capitalism or via primitive communism? Our sympathies will depend on which of these we consider the less painful, ugly, and damaging to the human soul. The pity of it is that with the long-range view on both sides, the alternative would become unreal. A third way, still difficult, but far more humane, lies open.

In the past, backward and helpless countries were taught to take their first steps in the modern world by the brutal method of colonialism. The colonizing powers had no altruistic motives in the teaching part; as in the case of primitive capitalism and the working class, this was an inescapable necessity (the "dialectic" again) distasteful to the exploiters:

educated natives and educated workingmen were uppity and dangerous. And just as in time the working class was able to establish a claim that has completely transformed the face of capitalism in advanced countries, so the underdeveloped countries are bringing about a transformation in international relations and colonialism. The working classes still pay a price for being what they are, whether in capitalist or Communist countries—in advanced capitalist countries much less than in Communist countries. But in advancing Communist countries, the standard of living of the working classes is rising rapidly. Whether the workers as compared with the managers will ever be as well off in Communist or capitalist countries is one of the great debates. The price exacted from backward countries for being helped into modernity brings no profit to the helpers; on the contrary, it is a heavy drain: neither America nor Russia will ever recoup the smallest part of the billions distributed in foreign aid. The "price" is, or is supposed to be, the development of the economic and social system of the benefactor. The sensible thing for backward countries is to accept help from both sides, as many are doing, and to pledge themselves to neither.

The contest between America and Russia for the installation of their respective systems in new areas becomes even less intelligible from the economic point of view when we observe the behavior of the beneficiaries. As soon as they achieve some independence, they very properly act with an eye to their own interests. They trade where they can get the best terms, so that the benefactor is not even rewarded with a reliable subject market.

What, then, explains the policies of the rivals in the field of undeveloped countries? What are they up to with their respective "imperialisms"? Is it that unbelievable thing, idealism, operating in the international field? It is, alas, nothing of the sort. The millennium is not here. The driving impulse is mass egotism, the will to dominate, to impose one's group personality on others; mingled with it is suspicion, fixation in irrelevant attitudes of yesterday. I am not saying that no genuine issue exists; whether a backward country chooses the capitalist or the Communist transition is a serious matter, and it is probable that some countries are (as I would put it) doomed by now to pass through the Communist phase. But the issue cannot be resolved peacefully until the motivations on both sides are recognized for what they are, futile, distortive, and mortally dangerous.

The convergence in internal form of Russia and America is repeated in the convergence of intergroup relations within the two blocs. The notion that Communist countries are less selfish in their relationships toward each other is a survival, more marked among liberals than elsewhere, from what can only be called the gaga stage of Communist thinking. Capitalist countries will as a rule help each other more readily in their confrontations with Communist countries and vice versa, but that is part of the alliance; and of course the alliance is far less stable than it was twenty years ago. Who would have dreamed then of flirtations between France and Russia, America and Yugoslavia?

Imperialism of the old type, savage, conscienceless, defiant of world opinion, flourishes in Rhodesia and South Africa, but colonialism, where it lingers, is clearly on its last legs. Saudi Arabia, Iran, and the other oil countries of the Middle East are a case in point. They have not yet acquired the skills to run the wells for themselves, but they have learned to drive better bargains than in the past. When the right moment comes they will tell the West to get out, and the West will have to obey. But as a market the West will still remain indispensable. When in June 1967 the Arab countries threatened to stop selling oil to the West, they were making empty noises. The Talmud has a quaint argumentative phrase: "If he says that, he is saying nothing."

When American oil interests complain that American support to Israel threatens their investments in Arab countries, they too are saying nothing. The Arab countries will get rid of the American investors, or reduce their profits to an acceptable minimum when they have the strength to do so, and neither before nor after. That Israel is an instrument of American imperialism and colonialism is a point of view that has somehow failed to penetrate to the oil interests, which are notably anti-Israel. It may be argued that the irritant of Israel in their midst stimulates the Arabs to acquire modern methods, thus shortening the reign of the foreigner. To that extent, the oil interests have a case, but it is not one that they would care to urge publicly.

However badly American, British, Dutch, and Italian colonialism has treated the Middle East Arab countries, it is certain that Russia's recent intervention on their behalf has been the greatest calamity they have suffered in modern times. Instead of trying to open their eyes, so that they might see in Israel a Godsent opportunity, an unexpected regenerative force for the region, Russia took her cue from Nasser and made a pawn of Egypt, then of Syria, as ruthlessly as they in turn made pawns of the Arab refugees—all in the name of liberation from the yoke of Western capitalism. Nasser had some good ideas, but mixing them with bad ones he more than canceled their effect. Whatever little improvement he has brought into the life of the fellah has been paid for in blood, oppression, and asphyxiation. His ambition to become the leader of the Arab world, as well as the major power in Africa, had Russia's backing; here was something the Western powers would not like. What it did to the Egyptian masses had no place in the calculations of the Russian leaders.

But Nasser's frantic efforts to become the great leader ended in failure. His dashings to and fro, his dramatic appearances in various African settings, were without edible results. They got him no nearer to the oil of Saudi Arabia and Kuwait. There was some sense in his invasion of Yemen, which was to have become the beachhead for the invasion of Saudi Arabia. But he was still fighting there, with little prospect of an early victory, when he was plunged into the war with Israel. His prestige at that point was very low. There may have flashed into his mind the phrase so popular with the Communists at the time of the NEP: *reculer pour mieux sauter*. But it was only *pour mieux tomber*.

Had the war in Yemen ended in a quick victory, it would have proved that Nasser's propaganda among the local population had been effective. He could then have hoped for a similar victory in Saudi Arabia, although it was quite possible that the Saudi Arabians, having overthrown their rulers, would want to keep the oil for themselves. But there was no quick victory in Yemen. Thousands of lives were lost, and what for Egypt was a considerable treasure. The gamble was a poor one, and it canceled the meager economic benefits the masses had derived from the reforms. It did not improve their prospects of a human sort of existence. If there was some slight diminution in the economic gap between the classes, there was none in the social and psychological gap, which showed up horribly and disastrously in the war, and was one of the reasons for the shocking defeat. The officer class, drawn of course from the upper economic levels, was not simply incompetent; it had no feeling for the men in the ranks. On this aspect of the military operations all the correspondents are in agreement. The Israeli officer and his men are comrades in arms; they are often friends in private life. To the Egyptian officer, the man in the ranks is a faceless member of the lower orders. The handicap might have been overcome if the Egyptians had been fighting an invader. But given all the circumstances the Egyptian soldier was better than might have been expected. He went into battle without two indispensable accouterments: motive and self-esteem.

How was it that Nasser, with the experience in Yemen, did not understand this? He should have avoided war with Israel as one avoids the plague. He may not have known the strength of Israel's army; he should have known the weakness of his own. From the result some have drawn the conclusion that he did not want war with Israel. But it cannot be denied that he wanted what he could not get without war, and wanted it without waiting. We may also ask, how is it that the Russians were so ill informed on the comparative military strengths of Israel and Egypt? It is easier to believe that the Russians did not want war; if so, they are all the more culpable, for they could have stopped it. They chose instead to play at brinkmanship.

More correctly, they permitted and encouraged Nasser to play at brinkmanship, and perhaps a point was reached where they could not call off the game. It was not only the supply of arms. Nasser's vanity was fed to the bursting point by the plaudits of the Communist world, with Tito as cheerleader. But he is described as a level-headed man, in complete control of his emotions. If this is true, the blame shifts more heavily toward the Russians, and the evil they have done the Arabs stands out more darkly than ever. By egging on the Syrians to continuous incursions into Israel, Russia jeopardized Egypt's claim to leadership of the Arab world. To hold on as front runner Nasser had to do that which made war inevitable. He could not show himself less militant than the Syrians, or let them outbid him in the promise to annihilate Israel.

He kept the leadership, and as I write his hold on the Egyptian masses still seems so strong that one can speak of him and Egypt interchangeably. His manipulatory skill evokes a certain kind of admiration. At home he handled the debacle by convincing the masses that what Egypt had suffered was a "setback"—one might also call Waterloo a "skirmish"—and breaking off diplomatic relations with America for having, together with England, helped the Israeli air force. His guiding principle is: "Lie now, pay later"—with another lie; and he has to hope that the currency will not collapse.

This particular lie, though it served its purpose for the moment, was bound to annoy the Russians. It made them look like fourflushers. They could also challenge the usefulness of the lie; for if the Egyptians could not stand the idea that Israel was capable single-handedly of performing such an extraordinary feat, what good was it to tell them that she was helped by America and England while Egypt's great friend looked on idly or impotently? There were in fact some bitter remarks about Russian perfidy in the Arab press.

The Russians were also annoyed by being confronted with one of their own lies. "We all know," declared Nasser in his "resignation" speech, "how the crisis began. There was an enemy plan to invade Syria. The evidence was ample. . . . Even our friends in the Soviet Union told the parliamentary delegation which was visiting Moscow early last month [May 1967] that there was a calculated intention."

Though it was clumsy of Nasser to throw part of the blame on the Russians, they stood by their lie in the subsequent UN debates, then let it fade out. When the Russians accused Israel of making heavy troop concentrations on the Syrian border, a heated midnight conversation took place between Israel's prime minister and the Soviet ambassador. The Russian ambassador was invited on the spot to accompany the prime minister on a quick trip to the area, so that he might see for himself. The ambassador refused. I do not understand why. He could always have said later that he had seen heavy troop concentrations even if he had not. There seems after all to be a limit to Soviet mendacity.

Or is there? Listening to the UN debates after the war, hearing the stony-faced repetitions about Israel's aggressions, one began to doubt it. One needed iron nerves and a copper-lined stomach to listen for more than a few minutes at a time. And while this talk went on Russia was sending new shipments of planes and tanks to Egypt. Not a word about getting down to realities and initiating direct talks between the Arabs and Israel.

In private the Russian-Arab conversations were undoubtedly less harmonious than the public show of solidarity might imply. At the Khartoum Conference in September, Nasser was forced to deny publicly that the Americans and British had participated in the war. In general he took a more moderate tone, that is, he did not talk as big as before June 5. But all this amounted to was the admission that there was no immediate prospect of destroying Israel.

While we are on the subject of Russia's guilt, we would do well to remember that in the early years of the State of Israel none of the Western powers took steps to create normal relations between Israel and the Arab states. They were too busy with the cold war. Thus the abnormal situation hardened and became an accepted feature of the life of the Middle East. For nineteen years the Arabs insisted that they were still at war with Israel; hostilities were only partly suspended. The denial of the use of the Suez Canal to Israel was a continuous hostile act, and the raids into Israel were minor resumptions of hostilities. The United Nations adjudicated complaints within that framework and did nothing to change the framework itself. There were no pronouncements from the State Department or Whitehall or the Quai d'Orsay on the necessity of an Israeli-Arab accord. No Western statesman has told the Arabs bluntly: "Instead of calling for Israel's destruction you would do better to take her as an example."

Still, there is no comparison between the guilt of omission on the one side and the guilt of commission on the other. The Western powers did not want Israel's destruction. Perhaps Russia did not want it either, even after 1955. One may argue that Israel was some sort of asset to her, and the possibility of her destruction only a bait to the Arabs. But such devices have their nemesis. The Arabs saw not a bait but a promise, and when they tried to collect on it they ran into disaster.

Has Nasser learned a lesson? Can he retrace his steps, lift the ninth plague off his country, confront it with the truth, and make the Egyptians capable of self-government? He is credited with having had that dream once. Toward the end of his history *The Arabs,* written with great sympathy for the Arab peoples, and with considerable antipathy toward Zionism, Anthony Nutting has this curious passage:

> As a serving officer in the Arab-Israel war of 1948 Nasser realized how corrupt and ineffective was the leadership which the Egyptian monarchy offered to the Arab League in this first test of its combined strength. As the communiqués in Cairo kept announcing spectacular victories in battles which Nasser knew had ended in inglorious defeat, he resolved to get rid not only of the British but also the King and the corrupt politicians around him.

The king and the corrupt politicians are gone, the corrupt army has taken their place and the darkness lying on the land is deeper than ever.

[*Since the above chapter was written, Russia has penetrated more deeply into the slippery Middle East. The long-term value of that penetration is a highly debatable one.*]

15

Guidelines

As LONG as the Arabs consider the mere existence of Israel an act of aggression, everything she does must be wrong. The only good Israel is a dead Israel. But will the Arabs ever come round to the view of the first Feisal, that the Jews have returned to their homeland as of right? It would be childish to nourish that hope. Time will reconcile the Arabs to the existence of Israel. It is reasonable to hope that they will learn to benefit from her presence in their midst. It is unreasonable to hope that large numbers of Arabs will rise to the historic concept that called for Israel's restoration; least of all is it to be expected of the refugees. All they can see is that they have been miserably pushed around; their fellow Arabs may be much to blame, but it was the Jews who started it.

For the present Israel cannot hope to win over the Arab world by her decent treatment of her Arab minority and the Arab refugees. The Arabs of the surrounding countries will be isolated for some time to come in the world of fantasy created for them by their leaders. It is somewhat different with the Communist countries to which part of the truth penetrates, as the dissensions there witness. It is wholly different with the Western countries, where full reports are received and bias can be weighed against bias in public discussion. But Israel must act as though the truth were penetrating fully to the Arab and Communist countries.

The two most important principles that must guide her are self-preservation and fidelity to the best in her character. It may happen that, so guided, she will meet with an unfavorable opinion on the part of mankind. There is no help for that; only the unprincipled are guided solely by the criterion of public opinion.

The honest translation of principle into action is a difficult moral and intellectual exercise. There are individuals who would rather die than betray themselves; with them fidelity to character takes precedence over self-preservation. Can this be expected of a nation? The best elements in it may be heroic enough to offer themselves up; they may not be willing, they may not have the right to impose the same standard on others, on parents, wives, children. Suicide pacts can be made by a group, as at Masada; they cannot be made by a nation.

The principle of self-preservation may run amok and end up by defeating itself. The more a nation conquers in the name of safety the more enemies it makes and the less safe it feels. There is no end to it except by world conquest, an elusive aim not unknown in history. It is perhaps absurd to evoke this dilemma in speaking of Israel and her neighbors, but in her own small way she faces it.

The escape from the dilemma can be provided only by her neighbors, and they will do this when they are finally convinced that she cannot be defeated in war. It follows that every time Israel successfully repels an attack she must so strengthen her position as to offer less temptation to another attack. The justice of this formula is proved by the furious and futile insistence of the Communists and Arabs that Israel was the aggressor in June 1967. It was and is the ostensible basis of their demand that she withdraw to the positions she held on that date, as it was of the Arab demand in 1948 that she withdraw to the frontiers marked out by the UN in 1947. But it is pointless to speak of the Arab demand, the basis of which is the desire to destroy Israel.

The disposition of the Golan Heights, of the Gaza Strip, of Sinai, of the West Bank, must be subject to this formula. Not that the application of this formula is simple, either; for the physical security of Israel is not just a matter of frontiers and military position. It is bound up with the Arab population she has taken over.*

For the first time since 1948 the vast majority of the Arab refugees are within the territory Israel controls. With them are the Arabs who did not become refugees in 1948. The following are the approximate figures: there were 300,000 Arabs in prewar Israel, well integrated into her economy. The population of the West Bank was 850,000, that of the Gaza Strip 350,000, that of the Golan Heights 120,000. Some 330,000 Arabs fled from the conquered territories, and an undetermined number returned to the West Bank. The present (winter 1967–8) population of Israel is therefore approximately 3,800,000, of whom 2,300,000 are Jews and 1,500,000 are Arabs. Of the latter, about 500,000 are the refugees maintained wholly or in part by UNRWA.

Except for the practically uninhabited Sinai and the Golan Heights, negligible in extent, the new territory held by Israel fills out that part of Palestine which was left after Transjordan was removed from the application of the Balfour Declaration.† Territorially we are back at 1922, with enormous differences. Nearly 4,000,000 people live where less than 1,000,000 lived then; 500,000 are the recipients of an international dole but can be made self-supporting. And

* See map, page 6.
† See map, page 3.

the country is by no means overpopulated. Such has been the effect of the Zionist effort. But a greater difference thrusts itself on our attention. Where the Jews were a minority of one eighth or one ninth they are a majority of nearly two thirds. The greatest difference of all is in the world's acceptance of the State of Israel and the position it has won for itself in the regard of the world's progressive elements.

If we speak of prewar Israel without the Left Bank (but keeping the Gaza Strip, which cannot be detached) the Jewish majority is over seventy-five per cent. But twenty-five per cent is a substantial minority—twice as large as the Arab minority that Israel has handled very well hitherto; and a one third minority, if the Left Bank is included, raises serious problems outside the economic and civic field.

It is so obviously in Israel's own interest to raise the standard of living of her new and old Arab populations that the subject does not seem to call for discussion. But we have seen that within the Jewish population itself there is a sector, the Oriental Jews, which is at an economic disadvantage. This is only in a small part due to discrimination, and the discrimination is itself in part due to the difference in economic levels. The Oriental Jews came from countries backward in modern skills, and though an individual here and there may overcome the handicap, a community has a corporate inertia which is an additional handicap. Israel's treatment of her prewar Arab minority has called forth more criticism in Israel than in the outside world—a welcome sign that Israeli critics have the higher standards. If Israel does as well by her new Arab minority as by her old she will be doing very well indeed.

But the surrounding Arab world intends to make Israel's task as difficult as possible. The refugees of the 1948 war have been encouraged for nearly a generation in the hope that they would return to Israel as conquerors. Now they are in Israel as the conquered. Those Arabs of the West Bank who are not refugees have been subjected for the same period to a similar propaganda of resentment and hatred, and they too are within Israel's jurisdiction. And the propaganda continues, punctuated by acts of sabotage and murder. Israel must be prepared to endure much provocation and damage, she must deal firmly with each case as it arises, she must always bear in mind that her Arab neighbors are still at their old game—the provocation of a spiraling vendetta. They failed when the Arab minority was twelve per cent of the population. They hope to succeed with a twenty-five or thirty-three per cent Arab minority. If they do succeed, if they make it impossible for Jews and Arabs to live together in Israel, they will compel the Jews to defend themselves by firmer and firmer methods, perhaps, in the end, even expelling considerable numbers of Arabs. Again, no one will be the gainer. Thousands of new refugees will become the reluctant guests of their political exploiters, the Middle East will have taken a step backward, and its moral development will have received a severe check.

In general, the more than a million Arabs who have been taken over by Israel have been startled by the treatment they have received. Knowing that an Arab occupation of Israel territory would have been accompanied by a bloodbath, many of them expected the worst when the reverse happened. The promptings of their own consciences were reinforced by the wild propaganda that represented the Israelis as monsters and the condition of Arabs who remained in Israel as that of maltreated serfs. Thousands of Arabs from the West Bank and the Gaza Strip have visited other parts of Israel. They have seen the reality and they have begun to understand what deception has been practiced on them by the Arab governments.

Those who witnessed the mingling of Arabs and Jews when the walls of Jerusalem were breached, and the two populations flowed naturally into each other, recall it as one of the most moving episodes of the war, and this is what makes the Russian "eyewitness" descriptions of the occupation of Jerusalem particularly odious. Arabs streamed as freely into Jewish Jerusalem as Jews into the Old City. It is not necessary to exaggerate and to pretend that Arabs were happy to come under Israeli rule. But they were immensely relieved and astonished by the atmosphere about them. There were no grim faces, no scowls and insults and jostling; the attitude was one of downright friendliness. Within the Old City the shops were jammed with Jewish buyers, and stocks were emptied within a few days. The same scenes were enacted in Bethlehem and Hebron. It was a great novelty for Jews to be able to go shopping in Arab territory, and they bought vast quantities of rubbishy things, most of them imported, just for the fun of it.

There was more in it than novelty and curiosity. There was a conscious will to make friendly contact, to show that the enmity toward the Arab governments did not extend to the Arab people. The truth is that the Jews are not good haters, and well for them that it is so, for with so much occasion they would by now have eaten themselves up with hatred. In the Bible only one unimportant people is unforgiven, the Amalekites, of whom it is written: "Remember what Amalek did unto thee by the way as ye came forth from Egypt, how he smote the hindmost of thee, all that were enfeebled in thy rear . . . thou shalt not forget." But Egypt and Assyria are reconciled with Israel in the famous passage in Isaiah, and the Jews are bidden to cherish strangers because they themselves had been strangers in the land of Egypt. As for the arch-enemy Haman, he has become a comical rather than a sinister figure in the Jewish memory. A spasm of national hatred followed the unprecedented crime of Germany against the Jews; it has subsided into sadness. It is in the tradition that the Jews should harbor no hatred against the Arabs. And yet it seemed almost unnatural on the morrow of such a deadly threat to the existence of Israel not to hear anywhere a single expression of desire for punishment or revenge.

No obstacle exists on the Jewish side for a peaceful and fruitful Arab-Jewish integration. There are grave problems, especially if the West Bank becomes a permanent part of Israel; but they do not arise from Jewish hostility toward the Arabs, nor, for that matter, from Arab hostility toward the Jews. They will in fact come to the fore as the result of a peaceful accommodation.

They are not new problems. They were long and hotly debated before there was an Israel with a Jewish majority. They were theoretical then because, being in a minority, the Jews were not in a position to implement the program urged by one of the sides in the debate. An influential group of idealistic Jews regarded the creation of a binational state as the only just and practical solution of the Arab-Jewish problem in Palestine. The Arabs, then a large majority, and the proposed partners to the match, rejected it as a piece of Jewish *chutzpah*. Now a minority, they may be willing to consider it.

A binational state may be conceived of in many ways. Prewar Israel may enter into a union with the West Bank that would be more than a federation. They would have separate parliaments and a higher parliament in common. The Arabs living in prewar Israel might remain Israeli citizens, electing their representatives, as they have been doing until now, to the Knesset, or Israeli parliament, and enjoying national minority rights. Or they might become West Bank citizens electing members to the West Bank Arab parliament. Either way the two sections of the binational state would be joined in a customs union and a common currency. Foreign policy would be the business of the higher parliament. An extremely difficult, in fact an insoluble problem would be that of the armed forces. Could there be a single army with separate units, as in the old Austrian multinational state? Could the Arab section of the binational state have any army at all for a long time to come? The only likely wars would be with neighboring Arab states. Hitherto Arabs have not served in the Israeli army and very few have wanted to. The Druzes have served willingly and have been excellent soldiers, but they do not consider themselves Arabs, or if Arabs, a group apart in unfriendly isolation.

Another concept of the binational state goes much further. It calls for complete fusion, one citizenship and one parliament. With Arabs more than a one third minority the name of the state would have to be changed, perhaps to "Palestine," (which would be fair enough, since Palestine—*Philistia*—means neither Arabs nor Jews). The two languages and cultures would flourish side by side. Neither side would have privileges or duties beyond those inherent in enjoyment of the separate languages and cultures. The Arabs would be entitled to draw on the national budget for the creation of universities and institutes of higher learning—there are none at present—without regard to the taxes they pay. Presumably, though this has not been thought through, there would be one army, one air force, and one navy. There has been no discussion as to whether the parliament would be bilingual. Neither is it clear whether the fusion is to take place in a single act or by stages, and if by stages over how long a period.

All these proposals were once put forth with great earnestness and with good intentions. They must be examined—especially those that propose complete fusion—in the light of what the Jewish state has hitherto represented to its creators.

I have tried to show that something greater than the rescue and rehabilitation of Jewish refugees has been at the heart of the tremendous Zionist effort. A mighty tradition gave it endurance, drive, and character. The democratic and progressive spirit that permeated it and found incorporation in the Jewish state came with undiminished vitality out of the remote past. The East European Jews who made up the bulk of the neo-Zionist movement and provided most of its leadership drew on the Bible for their inspiration and on modern libertarian ideas and techniques for its implementation. They wanted the Jewish homeland to be the specific expression of the Jewish ideal and the source of Jewish renewal throughout the world. They believed that the fulfillment of their ideal would be a blessing to the surrounding peoples. But they did not return to their homeland in order to Hebraize the Arabs or to be Arabized by them. The source of their strength as well as of their high social program was their Jewishness.

The will of the Jewish homeland to remain Jewish has given fresh vigor to an old slander, that Judaism and Jewishness have a racist foundation. The slander is older than Christendom; but while the ancients may be forgiven for it, being ignorant of the Bible, the Christians cannot, their knowledge of it being thorough. They know that the two outstanding men of the Jewish Bible married out of the people: Moses, a Midianitess, and the daughter of a pagan priest at that; David a Hittite woman. Neither was rebuked for bringing "alien blood" into the folk. David was rebuked and punished for the murder he committed to obtain Bathsheba; but from their union Solomon was born to continue the messianic line. David himself was the great-grandson of Ruth the Moabitess, one of the most lovable figures in the tradition. The most ancient laws made provision for intermarriage, and the Israelites in the wilderness were bidden to take wives to themselves from among the Midianite women after the victory over Balak. All this is known in the Christian world, but the racist slander persists. The truth which lies on the surface, that the Jews were concerned with their cult, not their genes, has been deliberately obscured. The Nazis have been partially exonerated because they are supposed to have got their racist ideas from the Jewish Bible, though they themselves would never acknowledge an indebtedness to the Jews. Now a new darkness is cast upon the subject: the State of Israel is racist because it wants to remain Jewish. And how disheartening it is to hear this from lips of the outspoken racists among the Negroes.

There are small but highly articulate groups in Israel that want more than complete political fusion. I shall call them the Canaanites, though the name properly belongs to a particular group with irrelevant peculiarities. The Canaanites (according to my use of the term) consider Israeli Jewry the ingredient of a new ethnic entity unconnected except by outlived historical ties with the rest of world Jewry. The Palestinian or Canaanite people-to-be has its own destiny, which is neither Jewish nor Arab, but despite the name something new under the sun. The Canaanites as here described must not be confused with a somewhat larger group which has one representative in the Knesset, advocating a cutting of the ties with world Jewry as a preliminary to an understanding with the Arabs, though in the end such a severance will produce the same result.

The binationalists—I shall speak only of those who hold or held the "extremist" view—reject completely the Canaanite party program. Among them will be found distinguished individuals devoted heart and soul to the perpetuation of the Jewish identity and tradition; to them the ethnic and cultural fusion of Israelis and Arabs into a new identity would be a betrayal of the trust reposed in Israel by Jewish history and world Jewry. In the binational state they have so long urged upon the Zionists, Jewish spiritual values are to be cultivated parallel with the renaissance it will stimulate in world Jewry. They hold, indeed, that only a binational state will save the Jews of Israel (or "Palestine") from developing the un-Jewish characteristics of a nation forever on guard against the pressures of a large minority in its midst.

But they must also contemplate the likelihood, or rather the certainty, that a binational state with a large Arab minority will soon reverse the relationship, and it is the Jews who will be the minority. The Jewish rate of reproduction in Israel is among the lowest in the world, the Arab among the highest. If there is one thing the Jews have wanted to escape from for two thousand years it is the minority status, which has been the precondition of all their sufferings. There have been Jewish Galut or Diaspora nationalists who have held the belief that Jewish minorities, granted minority national rights, could flourish in the Jewish spirit anywhere. They have pointed to the very fact of Jewish survival as proof. Wherever the Jews have been permitted to practice their religion and conduct their own schools—and that, even when accompanied by considerable persecution, amounted to a form of national minority rights—they have maintained the tradition. Only massacre and expulsion put an end to Jewish life. Had the Jewish national minority rights granted to the Jews of Eastern Europe after World War I been honestly observed in spirit and in letter, Jewish life would have flourished there as richly as in the past.

But of course Jewish national minority rights were never honestly observed in Eastern Europe. They were granted sullenly under the pressure of the victorious Allies, they were evaded as soon as the pressure was withdrawn. Then came World War II, and in Eastern Europe nothing remains of the old order. If the new order has brought benefits to national cultures, the Jews are excluded from them.

An independent Palestine with the Jews in a minority must be accepted as part of the binationalist program, not written into it, but inherent. That Jewish immigration will offset the Arab populational increase is out of the question. For the time being Jewish immigration is practically at a standstill. It will take time before the profound effect of the 1967 incidents will issue in a substantial immigration from the West, and then it will be too late, or the immigration will not be substantial enough. Besides, Israel, or "Palestine," has a limited capacity. When everything possible will have been done with the Negev, when agriculture and industry have reached their highest level of production, the country may accommodate two or three million more. After that, increase will have to be held down by birth control or migration.

The national rights of the future Jewish minority will of course be guarded by the constitution, which will guard those of the initial Arab minority. But constitutions are not laws of nature. Can the future Arab majority be trusted? The question invites a counterquestion: Can the Arabs trust the Jews? While they remain a majority the Jews too can change the constitution. The fear of being majorized may lead them to close off certain areas to Arab settlement and certain occupations from Arab employment.

The position of the Jews of Israel has one dominating feature: they are surrounded by an enormous Arab world. In the total picture they will always be a tiny minority. It is their hope that they will come to a creative accommodation with the Arab world by setting a social and productive example, by making Israel a radiating center of education, modernization, and expertise, of democracy and social justice. They have already done this to some extent, although, like certain diathermic machines, they have not reached the areas in immediate contact, but some at a distance, in

Africa and Asia. But the achievement has meant a continuous internal struggle. Israel has had its own Jewish undeveloped human areas to carry along. It also has those elements in the Jewish population that are ideologically hostile to democracy and social justice. A relatively small Arab minority within Israel, a minority unaffected by Israel's ideals, though benefiting from them, adds enough to the burden without a large Arab minority. What will be the effect on Israel's ideals when an Arab majority, still remote from her concepts of desirable human relations, will set the pace by passing the laws?

One may let oneself dream of a time when the Jews of Israel will have no struggle to maintain and advance their democratic ideals, when an Arab minority, small or large, will share those ideals; of a time when the surrounding Arab world will be not only reconciled to the existence of Israel but will also accept her as a valuable partner in their own common efforts to set their house in order and play a helpful international role. That time is not going to be brought nearer by loading Israel with a large Arab minority, let alone crushing her under an Arab majority.

We must not ignore a point of view held by considerable numbers of Jews that the physical survival of Israel should be our only desideratum. As they see it, she has no obligation to be better than other nations, to be an example and a shining light and that sort of thing. When the foundations of the homeland were being laid in the 1920's and the early 1930's, the Zionist congresses were rent by the debates on "quantity versus quality." On one side there was the cry: "Get Jews into Palestine as fast as possible. Forget those expensive and impractical social experiments." And on the other side: "We don't want to build a Jewish homeland that will be just another superfluous addition to the world's teeming nationalisms. To have survived so long for so unedifying a purpose would make a mockery of Jewish history." The fierce debate was in a sense academic. The only ones willing to endure the hardships of the early stages were social idealists. Their opponents and detractors in the Diaspora had to support them or dissociate themselves from the idea of any kind of Jewish homeland. They could not make the second choice and they had to look on in alarm and indignation while starry-eyed and impractical idealists created the *kibbutzim* and cooperatives and social services that imparted a decisive momentum to the growth of the Jewish homeland—so decisive that it even overcame the Hitler time, when everyone conceded that quantity had to take precedence over quality. But the efforts to discredit the social ideals of Israel have not ceased. They are still, they will no doubt always be, part of the problem.

In Israel physical survival and the survival of character are not as obviously in conflict as they have been at some points in the past. But they are not reconciled, they have only been moved to another field.

16

Assimilation and Israel

CANAANITISM is a special variant of assimilationism, which is a philosophy and phenomenon as old as the Jewish people, having been born simultaneously with it when the Torah was given at Sinai. The Torah was in fact being prepared for it above while below it was trying to assimilate, that is, trying to lose itself among other peoples. Assimilationism has many forms, some of which should be examined here.

The simplest form is hedonistic and can hardly be said to have a philosophy. A man with some remnants of Jewish identity about him finds them uninteresting and irrelevant to whatever he wants to be and do. Something nasty may happen to him as the result of a Dreyfus or a Beiliss case; then, like Swann in Proust's novel, he may discover that he is being charged with much more Jewish identity than he has. And then, like Swann again, he may suddenly feel that he belongs to the Jewish people and has nothing to belong with. Or, something thrilling will happen to him—he will be caught up in the great response to Israel's victory; then he is quite willing to be credited with more Jewishness than he has. What happens after that depends on many factors of character and memory. He may form a permanent attachment and cultivate it into a significant Jewish identity, or he may be content with a philanthropic gesture and an intermittent pleasurable sensation about his Jewishness. He cannot be said to have a philosophy either of assimilation or Jewishness, except insofar as we can give that name to a bundle of personal predilections.

There are three main philosophies of assimilation, with subdivisions: one is general, the others are of the Right and Left. All of them by definition are aimed at the disappearance of the Jewish people. The general philosophy regards Jewishness as an anachronism. It is inclined to the view that all group identities are anachronisms, the Jewish, however, more than any other. The all-human scene is the field of the general assimilationist's concern. Men everywhere should throw down the divisive walls of their group identities. Sometimes, like Pasternak in *Doctor Zhivago,* he says that Jews by their tradition are best fitted to lead the way, not perceiving that in bestowing this honor on them he is emphasizing their identity and placing them in a paradoxical position; for if they are the best fitted for this task they had better hold together until it is completed, and that will not be tomorrow.

The assimilationist of the Left is the revolutionary. For him the Jewish identity is something more than an anachronism; it is a bulwark of reaction. A Jew may be a secularist, an atheist, a radical, a (pseudo) Communist—as long as he insists on a corporate Jewish identity he is an enemy of the revolution. The Jewish problem will be solved when the new order, destroying the vested interests which are the cause of anti-Semitism, will remove the cement that holds the Jews together.

The assimilationist of the Right is the patriot who is offended by the suggestion that because he was born of

Jewish parents he is in any wise different from his non-Jewish fellow citizens. For him Jewish history is a curiosity, like the history of the Moabites, and though better known as remote from his interests; if he holds on to the Jewish religion he divests it of all ethnic or historical particularities which belonged to its primitive stage.

All three assimilationisms have their modifications, which are sometimes the natural outcome of social environment. Where Jews are numerous and assimilation is resisted by non-Jews, general assimilationists and assimilationists of the Right are confined to each other's company; they form Societies of Assimilating Jews and carry on an active propaganda against the Jewish identity, concentrating their fire on Zionism and soliciting membership from among non-assimilating Jews. General assimilationists and assimilationists of the Right are at odds on patriotism and religion. The latter are inclined toward religion because it has patriotic associations and also because to lack it sets one apart. General assimilationists are above patriotism but behave discreetly for fear of being denounced as Jews.

Where Yiddish-speaking Leftist and Communist assimilationists (there are such) are not held together by language, they may to some extent be pushed together from the outside even within their movements. We have just seen that in Russia the offspring of two Jewish parents must, willy-nilly, carry a Jewish passport and suffer the consequences. There and in other countries a *numerus clausus* operates tacitly in the Communist leadership, whether on anti-Semitic grounds or on tactical grounds issuing indirectly from anti-Semitism. The *Yevsektzia* was dissolved, after many of its members were liquidated, for reasons unconnected with Communist theory. As a nationality the Jews of Russia are obviously entitled to a Communist section of their own. This, however, is a privilege they are glad to dispense with, the non-Communists for obvious reasons, the Communists because it was an obstacle to assimilation. But while the dissolution of the *Yevsektzia* smooths the path to assimilation, Jewish Communists, for all their happiness, must feel themselves singled out for discrimination.

Not all Jewish leftists are assimilationists. The Jewish Diaspora nationalist movements were strongly tinged with a Leftism at war with the bourgeois and religious elements. Whether of the Left or Right, Diaspora nationalists were either opposed to Zionism or regarded the settlement in the homeland as only one of the many Jewish nationalist groups scattered throughout the world, without spiritual priority. This kind of Diaspora nationalism has practically disappeared, and with it the opposition or relative indifference to the Jewish homeland. Language was the principal battleground between the Diaspora nationalists and the Zionists, the former asserting that Yiddish is the language of the Jewish people, the latter insisting on Hebrew. It was a strange and pathetic conflict. Most of the Zionists, including the leaders, spoke and loved Yiddish while those of them that knew Hebrew, read and wrote it easily, but spoke it haltingly. Most of them going to the homeland had to fight down their Yiddish and learn Hebrew from scratch. Among the Diaspora nationalists the leaders knew and loved Hebrew and were steeped in its literature. The muddled conflict is now over. The early taboo on Yiddish in the homeland has long since been lifted. You no longer risk a public rebuke on the street or bus for talking Yiddish; Hebrew no longer fears the competition. Yiddish writers are honored at receptions, a Yiddish theater flourishes, Yiddish journals are published, one of them the best of its kind in the world. The Diaspora nationalists give preference to Yiddish but regard the Jewish people as bilingual. Above all they have become Zionists, and recognize in Israel the primary guarantee against assimilation.

The condition that once made Diaspora nationalism a

plausible theory has disappeared: large aggregations of Yiddish-speaking Jews supporting a network of Yiddish publications and institutions. These were to some extent the product of segregation; they grew up where Jews had been denied a share in the life of the host people and had therefore never developed a taste for it. Jews lived apart. In the Western world of today, Jews do not live apart and do not wish to. They are as deeply involved in the life of the host people as their fellow citizens. There are Jewish districts, but Jewish homes are penetrated by the culture of their countries; the radio, television, newspapers, and magazines enter as freely as into non-Jewish homes; the same political issues are discussed there, the same plays, books, personalities, and fads. The tone may be different; a Jewish enrichment is perhaps added. But the instruments that once sustained Jewish life in the Diaspora have been replaced by the Jewish homeland. Without this replacement there can be no Jewish survival.

Diaspora nationalists have been at one with Zionists in assigning a special civilizing mission to the Jewish people. In one sense they set even higher sights—it was their dream that the Jewish people could go on forever as an example of a national culture sustained by pure will without the instruments of territory and governmental authority.

The special form of assimilationism that I have called Canaanitism turns the clock back by about thirty-five hundred years, hence the appropriateness of the name. It proposes that the Jews who have returned to Israel because they failed to assimilate in the West should assimilate in the East, to which they belong. That is in fact what the Jews tried to do when Joshua led them into the Promised Land, and what they kept on trying to do, always failing there, too, because of the perversity of a minority misled by the prophets. To the "Canaanites," the Zionists are the modern reactionary equivalents of the ancient prophets; they want the Jews to go on existing as a people, and what is worse, as a peculiar people.

One may apply the term assimilationism to the view that Israel, while remaining a distinct ethnic and political unit, should stop thinking of itself as a peculiar people, a people with a mission. The Homeland was rebuilt so that the Jews in it might lead normal lives, and normal means ordinary. Israel is to be a normal and ordinary country, not unbalanced by a *Weltverbessungswahn*. But whereas in other countries Jews can assimilate only as individuals, here more than two million of them have a magnificent opportunity to assimilate in a mass action organized as a national policy.

An extremely important aspect of the assimilationist–anti-assimilationist debate hinges on the extraordinary contributions the Jews have made in the fields of science and of moral and social philosophy since their emancipation. Assimilationists accept the fact, but they see no loss to the world in the disappearance of the Jewish people. The abilities of individual Jews will be passed on through appropriate mates of any ethnic group; they will only be unidentifiable as Jewish. The assumption is that the Jewish intellectual tradition plays no part in the high incidence of Jewish achievement. An alternative assumption is that the tradition has penetrated to the genes; a biological type has been created and is self-sustaining without further inbreeding or fostering. The tradition has done its job and is now superfluous.

Both assumptions are unscientific, but that would not matter if they were not also harmful. For the Jew, an informed attachment to the tradition is a powerful intellectual and moral stimulus. This is especially true if the attachment is formed at an early age. A knowledge of Jewish history provides a unique insight into the nature of the moral struggle; or perhaps the plural should be used, for the Jew struggled internally with his own weaknesses while he struggled with the external world. And since the intellectual and the moral are closely intertwined for the Jew, Jewish history also provides an insight into the nature of the intellectual life and the problem of its cultivation under adversity.

The type of assimilationism that calls for an "ordinary" Israel assumes that an "ordinary" world Jewry will support it. But neither an ordinary nor an extraordinary world Jewry would be interested in an "ordinary" Israel. The interaction between Israel and world Jewry takes place against the background of the tradition. For the modern Jew, even when half assimilated, is only a generation or two removed from forebears who carried the tradition. The dominant progressivism of the modern Jew owes much, but not everything, to the liberation he received from progressive forces, to the sufferings he endured at the hands of reactionary forces. His higher intellectual standards, which have been threatened of late, owe everything to the tradition of his own people.

World Jewry would be puzzled and repelled by an Israel that is not in the forefront of the world's peoples socially and intellectually. The feat of arms Israel performed in 1967 would have lacked most of its appeal if Israel were not pacific, progressive, and intellectually minded. Some Israelis may protest, "We are not here just to make you feel good," and others, "If you will not join us here, we do not care what you call yourselves and how deeply attached you are to the tradition." But the dominant feeling as I sensed it in the summer of 1967 was one of immense joy in the renewal of the bond with world Jewry, and world Jewry reciprocated.

The psychological and spiritual consequences of the renewed intimacy will work themselves out slowly in world Jewry. Between the shock of self-discovery and the exploration of its possibilities there will be an interval of doubt, of unwillingness to follow through. The willed remaking of a personality is an arduous enterprise, and laziness is a powerful deterrent. But it has happened before in Jewish life—we have been watching it happen during a half century of Zionist history.

It is futile now for Arabs to say that they are not anti-Semitic, they are only anti-Zionist. The number of non-Zionists is dwindling. If pride in Israel and readiness to help her are enough to make a Zionist—and they are in Arab if not in Zionist eyes—the large majority of Jews are Zionists today. In any case the distinction between "Zionists" and "Jews" is made by Arab spokesmen only in more prudent moments. *The Protocols of the Elders of Zion* is standard reading among the Arabs, who do what they can to bring it back to the attention of the Western world. *The Protocols* has nothing to say about Zionism; its subject is Jewry's alleged conspiracy to destroy Christian civilization, and since it was written primarily for Christian consumption, the Moslems were overlooked. The Arab effort to set off a new wave of anti-Semitism in the Western world is an oddly self-defeating strategy; for if successful it would bring Jews to Israel sooner and in larger numbers than by the spread of authentic Zionism.

The Arab propagandists, however, may hope to offset the effect by winning Christians to their side in the political struggle, and there is, as I shall argue below, a connection between anti-Semitism and anti-Zionism. In any case they are trying to array the Arab world against the Jewish world, and the greatest damage they can do is to waken a general anti-Arab feeling among Jews. Their chances of success are very small; in this matter too world Jewry and Israel will be at one. World Jewry has in its way as great a stake as Israel in the peaceful settlement of the Arab-Jewish conflict; a failure will in the long run undermine the moral self-esteem that keeps it in the progressive camp, and turn Israel itself into a source of moral decline.

17

The Diaspora of the West

VISIBLY and vocally anti-Semitism is at a low ebb in the Western democracies and semi-democracies. Hitler has made it so disreputable that all but the extremest reactionaries, who have no reputation to lose, shy away from open association with it. Only the extreme Negro left is vociferously anti-Semitic and anti-Israel, and here Arab propaganda has scored its greatest success. It is a dangerous success. Exploited further it will lead to a new Christian-Arab hostile confrontation like that of centuries ago. The Negro adoption of "Moslemism" is, in passing, one of the marvels of history. The Moslem record in the Negro slave trade is as bad as the Christian, and longer; the recent massacre of Negroes in the Sudan by the ruling Moslems put a ghastly climax on the record; and the American Negro in revolt marches against his brutal Christian oppressors under the banner of his more brutal Moslem oppressors. On the banner is inscribed the device: "Down with the Jews."

As a revolutinary appeal the device is extraordinarily clumsy; the revolutionary elements in America, such as they are, wince before it. As an appeal to the quiet anti-Semitism of American Christianity it is ill-timed. The Jews of America are enjoying a vogue. They occupy a leading place, perhaps *the* leading place in literature and the drama, and amidst the immense popularity of Jewish books and plays "Down with the Jews" grates on the ear. Negro anti-Semitism is a tragedy where it is grass roots; where whipped up as strategy it is a folly as well as a crime.

But the current popularity of Jewish books and plays, that is, books and plays written by Jews on Jewish themes, has a special character that throws a disturbing light on Jewish life and Jewish-Christian relations. Almost without exception these books and plays deal with the Jewish past, and do so in a way that waters down the distinctiveness of the Jewish branch of civilization and leaves the false impression of a better understanding between Jew and Christian. The best illustration is *Fiddler on the Roof,* a musical comedy that has become a sociological phenomenon.

Most popular Jewish books and plays deal with the Jew of yesterday in America; *Fiddler on the Roof* deals with the Jew of yesterday in Russia. Despite the lightness of its form it aspires to a serious portrayal of Jewish life under the Czars, and its lightness and seriousness are equally appreciated by the public. But what it offers is as much of that life as can be understood by a Jew or Gentile who is fortified against an understanding of Jewish life. That it therefore completely traduces Sholom Aleichem, on whose material the play is based, goes without saying, but that is not important. It traduces Jewish life.

It is enough to examine the central character, Tevye the dairyman, in whom Sholom Aleichem has created the everlasting Jew in his Russian-Jewish incarnation. Tevye is the folk Jew, simple but intellectual, not devout but religious through and through, not a scholar but not unlearned. As Sholom Aleichem portrays him he wrestles with man's eternal moral problems and confronts God with love and expostulation, with adoration and wry humor. He does so in a Jewish context, with apt quotations from the sacred writings, Bible and Mishnah and Prayer Book, and expresses his rebellion by following each quotation with a disastrously comical and disrespectful mistranslation into Yiddish. At every such mistranslation the average Yiddish reader, also neither a scholar nor unlearned, must put the book down and laugh heartily—and gratefully. This is just what he needed—an escape from bitterness into laughter without an escape from Jewishness and God. The true human relationship between Sholom Aleichem and his readers depends on a common background of Jewish knowledge. In *Fiddler on the Roof* an attempt is made to reproduce the relationship against a background of common ignorance. The assumption, correct enough, is that the audience has a minimum knowledge of the Bible and none at all of the other Jewish sacred books. The closest approach of the stage-Tevye to his original is with, "As the Good Book says, if you spit in the air it falls back on your face"—a piece of vulgarity born of the playwright's assurance that the most hopeless ignoramus will be suspicious of the attribution. The pathos and grandeur of Tevye's faith, his profoundly wise and Jewish humanity, the tears in his laughter and the laughter in his tears, are replaced by a kind of sentimental and illiterate buffoonery.

I shall be charged with a lack of humor. A musical comedy is not a sociological study, and only a pedant will look for Jewish values in *Fiddler on the Roof*. Perhaps so, although I consider *My Fair Lady* a sound sociological study as well as excellent entertainment. But *Fiddler on the Roof* has been tremendously acclaimed precisely because, in spite of its lightness, it is supposed to be a faithful rendering of the spirit of Russian Jewry, and, in a way, of Jewry generally. Apart from which one hears on every hand that the play is good public relations—it makes non-Jews like Jews.

It certainly makes Jews look like non-Jews, but what non-Jews like in *Fiddler on the Roof* is not the Jewishness of the Jews, for it is not there.

The values of contemporaneous Jewish life do not interest the Jewish writers now to the fore; this is not a fault in them, but their depiction of the Jewish life of the past betrays gross ignorance. In contemporaneous portrayals it is made to appear that Jewishness is unrelated to Jewish knowledge, and "the tradition" consists of the simple awareness of being a Jew. Again, I do not hold it against these writers that they have no feeling for Israel; I hold it against them that they ignore the place of Israel in Jewish life. Perhaps they will before long be compelled to deal with it. In *Fiddler on the Roof* Tevye is shown at the close of the last act preparing to leave for America; in Sholom Aleichem he prepares to go to the Holy Land. If the play had been written after June 1967 it might have been found better theater to stay by the original version. Sholom Aleichem, as it happens, was a Diaspora nationalist no less than a Zionist. But he was an incorruptible artist, and although Tevye never reached the Holy Land, the longing for it was bound to rise uppermost in his heart when he was left alone in the world. He is so far denaturized and de-Judaized in the play that the idea does not even occur to him. And I cannot close these observations on *Fiddler on the Roof* without mention of the rabbi, who in Sholom Aleichem is one of the most moving and most gracious Jewish figures ever created by a poet, and who in the play emerges as a rickety half-wit whose only contribution to the portrayal of the vast and manifold Jewish tradition is to bless a sewing machine.

Fiddler on the Roof is successful commercial literature; that is the only "defense" that can be put up for its inadequacies. But it does not mitigate the harmful effect of the play, which is a weakening of the prospect of a Jewish-

Christian understanding. And as a defense it is rather like an attorney's plea to the jury: "Ladies and gentlemen, my client is only a pickpocket, what do you expect of him?"

The same plea cannot be made for the higher level of American Jewish writers who have captured the attention of the critics and of much of the reading public. We shall look in vain among these for data which would help us define or feel the Jewish identity. They have, moreover, so concentrated on that segment of Jewish life which is least Jewish that theirs may be defined as the "literature of the Jew who isn't." This is natural; they themselves belong to that segment, and their work is artistically honest except when they try to evoke the tradition. The Jew who finds the characters in these books almost uniformly unpleasant must not blame the author. The picture of Israelites at work becoming Canaanites, Judeans becoming Greeks, Irishmen becoming Englishmen, Polynesians becoming Westerners, anyone trying to become someone else for the sake of convenience, or under pressure, is never a pleasant one. Assimilations of peoples must always go on, old peoples must die so that new ones can be born. But the process of assimilation, the transitional time, with its half-personalities, is a sad one. Thus Latin is a great language, so is French; but Latin becoming French is barbarous.

It is pointless to object to books by Jewish writers in which we meet only unappetizing half-Jews, though it should be added that as a rule the writers go out of their way to add a gratuitous touch of nastiness to their characters. Taking this body of literature as a whole, a Jew who is warmly related to Jewish life must ask, "But where am I? And where are my friends and acquaintances, the Jews who occupy themselves with Jewish education, synagogues, philanthropies, refugees, Israel, Russian Jewry? These interests of ours don't make us less human; apart from them, and as part of them, we have problems, tragedies, crises of conscience, virtues, and, what is more important for the writers I am talking about, meannesses and absurdities aplenty. And, since this seems to be a literary *sine qua non,* we too sometimes use dirty four-letter words. Don't we rate a corner of the canvas?"

An anti-Semitic character in Joyce's *Ulysses* asks of Bloom, the all-but-assimilated Jew, "Is he a Jew or a gentile or a holy Roman or a swaddler or what the hell is he?" One need not be an anti-Semite to ask this question of the half-Jews who fill the popular American literature of our time, and of the men who produce it; one may ask it in all friendliness. Or one may not ask it at all, being content with the impression that this is the Jew; which brings up another important question: why are these books so popular? Is it their literary merit? We know that popularity and literary merit rarely coincide; if they always did, every age would be bursting with good literature. There are always many popular books, few good ones. Fashions and fads seem to be the explanation, often inexplicable. But in the present case the explanation lies at hand: a general interest in the Jews, part of the backwash from Hitlerism. The interest is benevolent, lazy, and evasive. It does not strive for a knowledge of Judaism or of Jews in their Jewish capacity. And most Jews are content and are themselves avid readers of this literature. The vague reaction is: "It doesn't matter, as long as they're nice to us." But it matters a great deal, though only the educated and self-respecting Jewish minority perceives it. It also perceives that a genuine understanding between Christian and Jew is impossible before a much larger body of educated Jews has been created.

The Jewish education of the American-born Jew has only recently been given serious attention, and the greatest obstacle facing educators is the wide-held belief that to acknowledge oneself a Jew constitutes all of Jewishness. The bare preliminary is taken for the vast totality, and

Jews who are psychologically committed in some faint degree feel that they can dispense with the spiritual and intellectual commitment. The error is compounded when the psychological commitment fulfills itself completely in contributions to Israel or to some Jewish philanthropy.

For the majority of Jews the commitment will always be more psychological than spiritual and intellectual. It is idle to dream of an American or any other Diaspora Jewry completely and deeply versed in the Jewish tradition. But a healthy Jewry has to possess enough of the tradition to become aware that its predominantly progressive and intellectual character has been largely bequeathed to it: that the line of transmission goes much further back than the recent past, further back than the Exile experience, back to a choice made by a remote ancestry in the territory now called Israel. Such a Jewry must know that its ethic and its intellectual ardor, threatened but still persistent, were infused into the people thousands of years ago and perpetuated from generation to generation. The perpetuation was conscious, systematic, disciplined. The tradition was not, and is not, in "the nature of the Jew." It had to be renewed from father to son by arduous effort; if the effort is relaxed, the character will die. Or rather, the relaxation is the portent of death.

As the choice was made in Israel thousands of years ago, so the reaffirmation of the choice throughout Diaspora Jewry is linked with the reaffirmation in Israel today. The two Jewries rise and fall together according to their common application of the tradition to the solution of their problems—general social problems, the problems of Israeli and Arab relations, of relations between Occidental and Oriental Jews, between Negroes and whites, between the Western world and the Arab world.

An American Jewry sufficiently recharged with the tradition will turn from the literature it finds so attractive today, and the change in demand will bring forth—it has already begun to bring forth—a new literature. Such a Jewry will also be dissatisfied with a Christian-Jewish pseudo understanding. Only adolescents of all ages would rather be liked than understood; a mature and self-repecting people wants a deeper exchange with other peoples. The value of the exchange lies in the useful study of dissimilarities; the all-human similarities are the basis of the understanding.

The growing recognition of the peoplehood of the Jews is only a recognition of similarity, and this is in itself an advance. Until Israel had penetrated to the consciousness of the Western world the Jews were regarded only as members of a religious body. As such, they were not entitled to the first attribute of peoplehood, which is the possession of their homeland. There was of course also a special reason for denying the Jewish people its homeland: its permanent dispossession was implied in Christian tradition; and even where Christian faith was weak, the tradition had passed over into the secular folklore of Christendom. In its transitional stage between the two world wars Reform Judaism acquiesced in this view, but, except for a remnant in an arrested stage of development, does so no longer. It is becoming clear that the denial of Jewish peoplehood and of Israel's right to existence, with all that it implies for the Jewish people, is rooted in anti-Semitism. That the old Reform Judaism should not have recognized this need not surprise us. In other areas, too, anti-Semitism has had a subtly demoralizing effect on Jewish thought.

There is still much reluctance to accept the existence of Israel tacitly and naturally, but we must distinguish between transient political motivations and deep-rooted ideological attitudes. We must also be careful not to confuse an unfriendly attitude toward Israel with a denial of its right to exist. When De Gaulle, having settled the Algerian problem, was free to woo the Arabs, he ditched Israel. This was dictated by expediency—and *l'honneur.* Expediency and *l'honneur* change from year to year. When Mao Tse-tung discovered Nasser, and later the Syrian leaders, he also discovered the usefulness of enmity to Israel. This too was dictated by expediency—and the salvation of humanity. (De Gaulle and Mao are illustrations of the law of history that every statesman wants to stay in office long enough to undo his own work.*) Russia's enmity may not be purely tactical, motivated as it is in part by anti-Semitism. In China's case, we cannot talk of a divergence of views on Israel between the leaders and the people; that the Chinese have ideas about Israel is not, to say the least, at all likely. But in Russia and the other Communist countries, ideas about Israel do exist, and they do not always conform to the ideas of the leaders. In France the distaste of the French people for the official policy toward Israel during and after the war was so general that even De Gaulle was unable to ignore it. In England, too, the government's stand and public opinion were at odds.

Throughout the Christian world the reluctance to accept the existence of Israel tacitly and naturally as the corollary of the peoplehood of the Jews is far stronger in the Church establishments than in the laity. Here the resistance is deeply ideological, though it may sometimes be used tactically. In the Second Vatican Council's "Declaration on the Relations of the Church to non-Christian Religions," proclaimed by Pope Paul VI on October 28, 1965, the passage on the Jews contains a curious and apparently uncalled-for aside that marks it off from the passages on the other non-Christian religions. The Declaration pays tribute to "the good things, spiritual and moral," to be found

* De Gaulle's anti-Israel and anti-Semitic statement to the press on November 27, 1967, is for the moment (December 1967) the latest instance of the law in operation, his subsequent "clarifications" notwithstanding.

in the non-Christian religions, as well as to their "socio-cultural values." " . . . in Hinduism, men contemplate the divine mystery and express it through an inexhaustible abundance of myths and through searching philosophical inquiry. . . ." " . . . Buddhism, in its various forms, realizes the radical insufficiency of this changeable world. . . ." "The Church regards also with esteem the Moslems. They adore the one God living and subsisting in Himself, merciful and all-powerful. . . ." The last and longest passage on the non-Christian religions is devoted to the Jews.

It will be remembered that this pronouncement was a great disappointment to most Jews and to a number of Protestants and Catholics. It seemed to them that in the light of what Christians have done to Jews throughout the ages, and more particularly after what happened to the Jews under Hitler, it was at best a feeble gesture and at worst evasive on the part of the Church to declare that the Crucifixion "cannot be charged against all the Jews, without distinction, then alive, nor against the Jews of today." They were also profoundly disappointed by the passage that "reproves" where it should at least have "condemned" "as foreign to the mind of Christ any discrimination against men or harassment of them because of their race, color, condition of life, or religion," and again by the generalizing of the problem of anti-Semitism in the passage: "Furthermore, in her rejection of every persecution against any man, the Church, mindful of the patrimony she shares with the Jews, and moved not by political reasons but by the Gospel's spiritual love, decries hatred, persecution, displays of anti-Semitism, directed against Jews at any time and by any one." And "decries" or "deplores" are scarcely the words for what should be considered a mortal sin.

In these criticisms little attention was paid, even by Jews, to the words "moved not by political motives" in the last passage. No such disclaimer appears in the fraternal greetings to other non-Christian religions. Its singular appearance here inevitably suggests *qui s'excuse s'accuse.* The only question is: What lies behind this politically motivated disclaimer of political motives? Which leads to the question: What political motives can the Church possibly be accused of when it "decries" or "deplores" hatred and persecution and displays of anti-Semitism? The desire to be friendly to the Jews (though not so friendly as to clear them once and for all of the hideous and superstitious charge of deicide, the key word avoided with great circumspection) is not going to be interpreted politically by Nazis and other anti-Semites. They may dislike it, while feeling relieved at its reserved tone; they are not going to say that the Catholic Church is intruding into the political field. Only one hypersensitive group is going to say it, and that is the Arab Christians who think they smell in the statement the possibility of future acquiescence in the existence of the State of Israel. And it will also be remembered with what similar circumspection the Pope, on his visit to Israel, avoided any hint of present acquiescence. We do not need accounts of what went on behind the scenes in order to know that the Arab bishops fought obstinately on the side of the conservatives for the emasculation of the stronger original statement and the inclusion of a political disclaimer.

The Church must not do anything that is likely to create a schism or drive large numbers of its flock from the fold. It feels it has gone far enough in naming anti-Semitism among the deplorable manifestations of an un-Christian spirit. But for the Arab bishops that was going too far, and so, moved entirely by political motives, they demanded and got the disclaimer of political motivation.

I have argued that acquiescence in the existence of Israel implies acquiescence in the peoplehood of the Jews. These twin concepts run counter to classic Christian doctrine both Catholic and Protestant (they also run counter to various other notions on the nature of the Jews, but that does not occupy us here). It was therefore natural for the Christian establishments to display a shocking indifference to the facts of the Arab-Israel conflict generally and the war in particular. The voice of the churches was not heard in the gigantic protest that went up in America and elsewhere against the monstrous intent of the Arab states to wipe Israel off the face of the earth. There was no denial of the right of Israel to live; there was only a failure to rise against the planned murder.

The ideological bias of the churches, Catholic and Protestant, was strongly evident again in the discussions of the political future of the city of Jerusalem. If the advocates of its internationalization had been divided between laymen and the clergy in the relevant proportions the arguments could be discussed solely on their merits. But why should the clergy be overwhelmingly for internationalization? What this sudden concern about the guardianship of the holy places? Since the time of the Crusades the churches have resigned themselves to the Saracen and Turkish possession of Jerusalem. When, in 1948, Jordan seized Jerusalem, which was to be internationalized under the UN partition plan of 1947, the churches were easily comforted. Moslems had been the guardians for more than seven centuries, with no harm to Christianity. Access to the holy places was assured to all Christians—and why should it not be when it paid so handsomely? That access to the holy places in Jerusalem and the West Bank—Hebron, the grave of Mother Rachel—was denied to Jews not only of Israel but of every other country did not disturb the equanimity of the Christians. But *Jewish* guardianship of the places—that is quite a different matter.

The genuinely nonpolitical parts of the declaration on the Jews are offensive in their connotation that the Jews need to be absolved of the crucifixion. The political part is offensive in its not-too-well hidden and self-exculpating affront to the State of Israel. The declaration as a whole mirrors a characteristic tendency toward reservations on the subject of Jewish relief from ancient disabilities. A feeling of impropriety is attached to the full acceptance of the Jews as the natural equals of Christians in all respects, and the Christian mind mutinies at the idea. Something must be kept as a reminder of Christian charity in admitting the Jews to equality, and this something is inevitably, and in a profound sense, a denial of equality. How craftily and with what fertile inventiveness prejudice evades discovery!

But this particular prejudice did not need to invent the support it receives from Jews whose sole interest in the Jewish people is that it should vanish as quickly as possible. Their ill-mannered intrusions into public discussion of Jewish affairs could be dismissed as a minor nuisance if it did not lead many Christians to take the view that if some Jews don't want to remain Jewish, it is wrong of other Jews to want it; and not only wrong, but actually un-Jewish. Wrong because it frustrates the Jews who don't want to be Jewish, and un-Jewish because the nice Jews, i.e., the "real" Jews, are the ones who are doing their best to stop being Jewish. Unfortunately, there are also Jews committed to the Jewish identity who are in the habit of inviting prominent "disappearers," as I call them, to air their views in publications and on platforms, while imploring them not to abandon the Jewish people in its unhappy plight. This is as futile as it is undignified. I have some valued friends among "disappearers." They would not remain my friends if they were in the habit of barging into the Jewish problem and telling Jews what to do as Jews.

The committed Jews who run after assimilating Jews, urging on them the duty and the spiritual advantages of remaining Jewish, are those whose commitment is purely psychological. If they were spiritually and culturally committed they would not feel so panicky, and they would find enough to do teaching the tradition to those who are psychologically prepared for it. The only harm assimilating Jews do us internally is to absorb energies better bestowed elsewhere, and for that we are to blame. The external harm is something; but that cannot be undone by arguing with assimilating Jews. Nor can we, on the other hand, conduct useful discussions with non-Jews who want us to assimilate, whether by religious or secular defection.

Among those assimilating Jews who won't leave us alone the Communists occupy the silliest intellectual position. But the silliness is stained with something darker, which is not removed by Communist protests against Russian or Polish or Czechoslovak anti-Semitism. Communist and Christian anti-Semitism resemble each other when they deny the Jewish people alone the rights of nationalism or peoplehood. Jewish Communists, however, have special reasons for holding their peace, or, in the Yiddish phrase, taking a mouthful of water, when the Jewish subject is mentioned. The malevolence of Communist countries toward the Jews in their midst and toward Israel belongs to the general Jewish tragedy; the role played in it by Jewish Communists belongs to the chapter called "Jewish Enemies of the Jewish People." The moral issue is painful, but it should not obscure the comicality of the intellectual aspect. One ought to be tongue-tied when one is hide-bound, but few Jews are tongue-tied, and the Communist least of all. He chants the old slogans with increasing fervor as their absurdity becomes increasingly evident. Judaism is a reactionary force! The Jewish problem, and all other problems, can be solved only by universal communism! Israel is a tool of Western imperialism! Arab nationalism is a liberating force! The cracked record seems to be made of indestructible material. And of course Israel must return unconditionally to the perilous frontiers of 1948. Marvelous to relate, the Jewish

Communists of Israel, like their Arab *tovarichi,* are free to express the same opinions, if that is the right word. Some of them, having actually broken loose, and really having opinions, have ceased to be Communists. Russia has read them out of the party.

Jewish Communists in America are no longer a factor in Jewish-Christian relations, and when they were it was by exaggeration of their numbers, as of Communists generally. What stands in the way of the right creative relationship is the reluctance of the churches, rather than of the laity, to get over the first hurdle, which is to recognize the similarity of the Jewish people to all other peoples. Once this is done, an appreciation of the dissimilarities, so much more valuable in their way, becomes possible.

One more condition must be fulfilled before that possibility can be unfolded to the enrichment of American life, and that is a great lifting up of Jewish cultural standards among American Jews. It must begin in the home, with parents participating, both for themselves and for their children; it must permeate the religious centers; it calls for secular institutions, like the community centers; it calls for an extension of the Jewish day-school system and of the Jewish-oriented summer camps. We cannot speak of the revival of Hebrew as the spoken language of the Jewish home—it was never that in the Diaspora or even in the post-Babylonian Jewish commonwealth—but it has always been the additional language of the cultivated Jew, the language of his prayers and meditations and of his literary activity. But the chief mainstay of the Jewish tradition has always been and must always be its organic attachment to the land of its birth and finest flower, and a renascence of the Jewish tradition in America will be authentic only when it leads to the gradual migration of some hundreds of thousands of American Jews to Israel.

This last, climactic part of the program has many bearings. It must not be regarded as a withdrawal, much less a repudiation. Voluntary, conscious of purpose, it must strengthen Israel as the servant of both East and West. An Israel unidentifiably absorbed into the Arab world has little or no value for it. An Israel solely an extension of the West—which is what the Arabs accuse it today of being—is a disruptive intruder. An Israel remaining itself in an Arab-Israel federation—and this is bound to come—and retaining its connection with the West through millions of Western Jews, can play a unique unifying role. In his letter to Chaim Weizmann, the Emir Feisal speaks of him as "a great helper of the Arab cause." This is the natural course of Zionism, to be resumed after a long, painful, and bloody deflection.

In lifting itself to a spiritual and cultural level from which such a migration will flow, American Jewry will at last be able to establish the right relationship with Christian America. I have said that the recognition of similarity is the basis for the study of dissimilarity. One speaks of the dissimilarity between an apple and a pear because they are both fruits. One cannot speak of the dissimilarity between an apple and a triangle. Once the peoplehood of the Jews is tacitly accepted, and with it the rights Jews have in common with other peoples, the special character of the Jewish people can be examined.

It is first of all a world people and a world observer. Whatever happens anywhere—or nearly anywhere—happens to some part of the Jewish people and is communicated to the rest. If humanity is trying to create One World, Jewry is the pilot plant. At the same time, in the tenacity with which it has held on to its identity for some three and a half millennia, it proclaims the vital principle that One World does not mean One Face.

The Jewish people is an ethical people; that is to say, a Jew who identifies with his people is aware that this identification implies an ethical obligation, even if he considers himself an atheist. Whether a believer or an unbeliever, he may not, and often does not, honor the obligation; and whether he is aware of it or not, that ethic is the product of the Jewish religion. In that sense there are no Jewish atheists *pur sang;* and what we call secular Jewish nationalism is deeply involved in the Jewish religion.

This peculiarity puzzles the non-Jew, and sometimes the Jew, too. The Western world distinguishes sharply between nationality or peoplehood and religion. The reason is that religion came to the Western world from the outside, whereas the Jewish people was born as a religion. Secular Jews accept the principle of separation of church and state for Israel; but their secularism is really a variety of the Jewish religion. Reform Jews too, certainly not secularists, accept the principle, and so do many Orthodox Jews.

The Western world will be ill at ease with the Jew until it takes up an affirmative attitude toward the Jewish Diaspora as one of its permanent component elements. It must see in world Jewry a uniquely useful influence toward the harmonization of the world's nationalisms. It will do so in proportion as Western Jewry renews itself through Israel in the Jewish tradition.

18

The Long View

THIS book probably will be read by few Arabs, and by none of them with sympathy. They cannot, as I have said, be persuaded that the Jewish people had the right to reconstitute its homeland in their midst and that they have been wrong to oppose it. But I am not writing to persuade or convince anyone; I am writing out of an irresistible impulse to testify.

It came over me in the days immediately following the war. It was at its strongest not when I wandered over the Golan Heights, or flew over Sharm el Sheikh, or circled the rock of Masada, and not even when I stood again, after a separation of twenty years, before the gray stones of the Western Wall, but when I sat at some corner café and watched the people streaming by. Such ordinary people, busy, busy, busy with ordinary affairs, housewives, peddlers, merchants, students, each intent on his own errand, a cheerful, homey, and utterly unheroic spectacle. A few weeks ago, I said to myself, they were together in the shadow of death; powerful forces devoted to their destruction were gathering about them on all sides but the inhospitable sea; and they were alone. In this immense world they knew themselves to be quite alone—these ordinary homey people. They were not paralyzed with fear nor hysterical with rage; they did not whimper nor implore help; they did not scream back at the screaming enemy; they did not fall into panic. Calmly they went about their preparation for the ultimate test, and when the moment came they rose to it in a supreme act of faith. In that moment none of them was found wanting; and, the moment past, they went back to their ordinary lives, these people whom in a kind of stupefaction I saw streaming about me.

Act of faith! The Spanish for it is *auto da fé*. What a ghastly reflection that the Inquisitioners thought *they* were performing an act of faith, and not the Jews who were letting themselves be burned alive, crying, as the flames and the smoke mounted to their flesh, "Hear, O Israel, the Lord our God is One." And no doubt these men and women willing to die in frightful anguish rather than betray their faith were in their daily lives as ordinary in appearance as these their descendants.

Not the fighting was the act of faith, but the manner of it, in which the people was as one, unfearing and unhating. They came out of it astounded by what they had done, not sure that they themselves had done it, needing time to take it in. They had not quite grasped it when I was with them, and had scarcely begun to ask themselves, "Will we have to go through this again? If not tomorrow, then the day after? And still again, on some other tomorrow?"

They say "still again" because defeat vanished from their minds long ago. They can no more conceive of death than their forefathers at the stake could conceive of life in apostasy. But must their foreseeable life be that of their still remoter ancestors, trowel in one hand, sword in the other?

The answer that comes from some of their neighbors is,

"Yes. We will never concede your right to be in our midst. We will never be reconciled to it. If it takes a hundred years, two hundred, we will dislodge you from the usurped territory that is ours. We will pledge our posterity to eternal enmity. If we will not witness your destruction our children will, and if not they, then their children's children. Justice and history are on our side. The whole Moslem world is with us, and the Moslem world has powerful friends. If we cannot destroy you at one blow we will destroy you piecemeal. With the help of these powerful friends in the field of world politics we will maneuver you back to the positions you held before the last war. Then we will force or maneuver you back to the position you held before that. And finally we will push you out completely."

We must not take these words lightly, but not at their face value either. Certainly most of the Moslem peoples are with Israel's Arab neighbors, and when not consciously or overtly intent on Israel's destruction, they condone it by acquiescing in the intermediate steps. And what is true of them is also true of the "powerful friends."

The prospect would seem utterly discouraging to a people unaccustomed to the long view. But the long view is the specialty of the Jewish people. I shall not speak here of millennia, though an Orthodox Jew would not hesitate to do so. It is enough to consider the span of the neo-Zionist movement.

Theodor Herzl foretold in 1896 that the Jewish state would come into existence in fifty years. He was wrong by one year. He had not the dimmest premonition of the cataclysmic upheavals that would make the world almost unrecognizable in that span of time. Nor did the men who gathered about him, men whose Zionism often predated his and came, unlike his, from the heart of the Jewish masses. They believed with him, perhaps not in the exact figure, but something like it. Let us assume that it was just a wild guess which wildly turned out to be right. The point is in the long view, not in the guess.

But are not the Arabs too taking the long view when they vow that within a hundred or two hundred years they will destroy the State of Israel? So it would seem. And yet there is a crucial difference. The effective long view is something more than farsightedness. To be effective it must be accompanied by a fervor that makes it a factor in shaping the future. How passionate and how enduring is the Arab will to destroy the State of Israel? Of what uncompromising and enduring need is it born?

The will is passionate enough in some quarters; the quality of the need is questionable. The destruction of the State of Israel is not a life-and-death issue for the Arab states, and though they proclaim it to be such, it would not even benefit them physically or morally. Granted that delusions are oftener the springs of action than objective calculation of gain, and even objective calculation—insofar as it is not itself an illusion—blunders as often as not. But delusions are psychological states which do not long outlive the circumstances from which they issue. The delusion of the Arabs that the destruction of Israel would at the very least bring a great benefit, whereas in reality it would mean the dead loss of a great potential benefit, is based on transient circumstances.

The first of these is their economic and technological backwardness. It has induced the kind of mental sickness which both seeks and rejects the therapy. We have seen that they want the help of the advanced world, which they admire and wish to emulate because it is advanced, and resent because it has abused their condition. They look upon Israel as the latest and most flagrant instance of that abuse, originating in the Western part of the advanced world. Israel's help is the last they will accept.

The second circumstance is bound up with the first. It is

the "humiliation" of their defeat by Israel. I call it an evanescent circumstance because, though the fact is permanent, the reaction to it is not. Advanced peoples easily get over military defeat. Germany and Japan no longer feel the humiliation of their crushing defeats, and can enter without embarrassment into alliances with the victors. It has been seriously suggested that before the Arabs can reconcile themselves to Israel they must defeat her militarily and thus regain their self-respect. The suggestion is grotesque. Arab self-respect must be based on more substantial grounds, constituted by Arab entry into approximate economic and technological equality with the advanced world. And once that has been achieved, the successful war the Arabs might be able to wage against Israel will no longer appeal to them.

In those Arab quarters where the will to destroy Israel is most passionate, or the most passionately expressed, the quality of the need that backs it is particularly suspect. The ferocity of the Algerian and Syrian leaders is a mixture of frothy revolutionary zeal and the ambition to take over the leadership of the Arab world. Given a revolutionary situation, a revolution is made by groups of resolute men united for a time in a common purpose. There are no such groups in Algeria or Syria, and in neither country is there a revolutionary situation, which consists of large masses ready to rise against an entrenched order. There was a revolutionary situation in Algeria when the French were there; it resolved itself in expelling them. Today there are no masses "ready to rise" either in Algeria or Syria. From all descriptions the masses in both these countries are as dispirited and lethargic as they are in Egypt. As for taking over the leadership of the Arab (and African) world, Algeria is too far from the center and Syria is too small. Also, "taking over" calls for men of stature. In the Algerian and Syrian leaders the need to destroy Israel, or at least to be the loudest in clamoring for it, is born of the obsession that this is the key to leadership of the Arab world. And so they outshout Nasser, who has suffered from the same obsession in a more controllable form. From every point of view, then, the need to destroy Israel is not primary with anyone except some of the original refugees. The whipped-up fury of the Arab mobs has no grievance against Israel to sustain it. The only authentic element in the Arab clamor over the refugees is perhaps a deep irritation; it is felt that the Arab policy toward the refugees has not shed luster on the Arab name; and again I must emphasize that this is not a reflection on the authenticity of the Arab nationalist movement, which is the expression of a universal human need.

The hope reposed by the Arabs in "powerful friends" is a vain one. The rivalry of America and Russia for a sphere of influence in the Arab world is a delusional hangover from the days when colonies and spheres of influence represented economic or military advantages. I have already referred to a parallel delusion—that democratic capitalism and so-called communism are creating different and irreconcilable forms of social organization. Both of these delusions are fading out, though they are still nourished by fears which create their own justification. These, in turn, spring from their own delusions. Each country feels that it will be more itself, America more American, Russia more Russian, in proportion as its presence is felt in other countries. Each wants to predominate. What for? I have already given the only answer I can see: in order to feel predominant. It is a "pure" motive without an ulterior purpose, and that, I have argued, is as unidealistic as dominance with a practical purpose.

But as things are today great powers cannot compete in direct confrontation for any kind of dominance by methods of violence. They do it indirectly, by participating in wars between small or weak peoples, by supplying them with the arms and military instructors, by egging them on against each other. Also, however, by sending in Peace Corps workers and industrial experts, as well as capital, either as investments or loans or grants-in-aid. The two methods, so opposite in character, are alike in their uselessness for the purpose they are intended to serve, which is the spreading of the cultural influence, the impressing of the national identity on other peoples.

How long will it take before these truths are accepted, and the first method is discontinued, because it is vicious as well as futile, while the second method is extended for its own sake as an international public service? Without attempting an answer we may make two assumptions: that the acceptance will come gradually and by sectional application, and that it will be helped forward by sectional pacts and accommodations. But it is very probable that even before an accommodation is reached in the Middle East, America (as well as France and England) and Russia will re-evaluate their interests in it. Jews and Arabs are at an impasse; the Jews cannot be pushed out, the Arabs will not negotiate with them as a self-understood presence in the Middle East. Those that support the Arab refusal to negotiate in that spirit prolong the impasse in the lingering belief that they can still get something out of it. Meanwhile there are many Arab leaders who, to change the figure, know that they have painted themselves into a corner and are praying for someone to lift them out of it. It may well come about that between them Israel and the Arabs will produce the first major area of accommodation between the Communist and democratic worlds, so that the Zionist dream of building a bridge between East and West will be realized in a far larger setting than it originally embraced.

If we measure by achievement rather than by time, the distance to an Arab-Israel reconciliation is much shorter than the distance neo-Zionism has covered since its all but unnoticed birth. It is not the last of the obstacles in the path of Zionist fulfillment, and though it looms so large today it is not the largest. We must take a still longer view, and in a much wider perspective, to get some measure of the challenges that Israel and world Jewry will yet face in common with all the peoples of the world. We must look beyond the time when Israel, politically and economically secure in its Middle East setting, will, in concert with world Jewry, have to continue the specific Jewish contribution to civilization.

The nature of that contribution may be defined as the purification of nationalism, the clarification by example of its universal creative function.

The word "nationalism" has an ugly ring today; let me substitute for it "regionalism," and add that the two ought to mean the same thing. I understand by "regionalism" the setting within which men become themselves, acquire a language which is something more than a primitive set of signals, are given their first cultural mold, develop in the arts their first nonutilitarian appetites; in other words, become civilized. Later they may acquire other languages and cultures, but their ability to do so will depend on the degree to which they become sensitive to their first language and culture.

All cultures are regional in origin. They spring from a particular way of life, rooted sometimes in a particular place, sometimes in a particular group. The region or the group is the culture-producing unit; it is a necessity of civilization; it also satisfies the human need to belong. In the reaction to the aggressive nationalisms of our time the need to belong is cried down as a weakness, a limitation, an atavism. It is held that fully developed civilized man should feel so strong a kinship with all mankind that he has no need of a particular kinship. But a man who has not in his formative years developed a particular kinship will be incapable of any kind of kinship; and a man who deliberately represses a particular kinship in the belief that he will thus feel a kinship with all mankind is in worse case than the man who never felt a kinship; he denaturizes himself and looks with scorn on all who will not do the same.

Regionalism is subject to two diseases: it may become cancerous and turn into super-regional nationalism, or anemic and turn into provincialism. It may also suffer from both diseases at the same time. In either or both conditions it is intolerant of other regionalisms. Instead of saying, "This is the best way of life for me," it says, "This is the best way of life for everybody." It cannot enjoy the diversity of the world, and feed upon it, as healthy regionalisms do, digesting what suits them, ignoring what does not. A cancerous regionalism destroys, an anemic regionalism has no digestive apparatus.

The spiritual crisis of our time lies in the disease of nationalism brought on in its new form by the threat to the world's culture-producing units. This threat, with its promise of infinite physical benefaction to mankind, is the new technological revolution which is spreading irresistibly in all directions, propelled by its own inner pressure and by outer suction. It has an accelerating, self-begetting momentum; every burst of speed produces a greater speed, and no one, with the exception of a few impossibilists, wants to arrest it. The differentiated ways of life which have given the world its cultural diversity are being overwhelmed in the tumultuous process.

In a world of standardized methods of production, of uniform field and factory and office behavior, what room or occasion is there for the regionalist or national pattern? What essential differences are there between automobile or chemical or steel or food-processing plants in America and Russia today, in China tomorrow? The plans, laboratories, machines, statistical charts, computers, formulas, all converge on one pattern, a world pattern. So do the physical motions of the workers. If man is what he does, must not this uniformity of doing lead to a uniformity of being?

The obscure terror of being humanly submerged in the technological tide is the special cause behind the intensity of nationalist mood in the world today. The more they see themselves becoming alike, the more the nations shrink from each other psychologically while asserting their diminishing individuality in aggressiveness; and as they are being drawn closer together in behavior patterns, they are being brought closer together spatially by the increasing rapidity of communication and transportation. This "irrational" nationalism is making nonsense of economic theories of international relations, and nowhere is this seen more clearly than in the Communist repetition of old-time "imperialist" accusations. There is of course much imperialism in the world, but it is as common to Communist foreign policy as to capitalist, and its primary source is not the search for markets or raw materials or even military security.

I have put irrational in quotes because the nationalist frenzy is only partly so; the love of that which gave a man his personality is as natural as the fear of seeing it obliterated in world uniformity. The irrational side is the hope of overcoming the threat by war, and it is doubly irrational because war today is the best example of a standardizing industry. We may put it thus: since the technological standardization of the world is inevitable and desirable in spite of its anticultural side effects, the nations in their fear of the side effects resort to the kind of standardization that most glaringly emphasizes them. Men have always been most alike when trying to kill each other, but when the weapons were primitive the return to the differentiated personality was easier. Today the weapons, which include highly sophisticated—and standardized—psychological devices, penetrate deeply and permanently into the personality.

The escape from this vicious circle lies in the cultivation of nationalism as something other than the product of man's activity in the pursuit of a livelihood. But how is this possible in the face of "the inevitable and desirable technological standardization" of the means of production? The answer is provided by technological standardization itself. As long as man must work more than a few hours a week to meet his physical needs, technological standardization is only in its primitive stage. Certainly man is what he does, and certainly if he is occupied for forty or even thirty or even twenty hours a week following a standardized physical and mental behavior pattern he will become spiritually standardized. He will lose his spiritual home, the place of his belonging, the source and guarantee of his selfhood. But making a living can and should become the least of man's occupations and preoccupations, which should be devoted to safeguarding his spiritual and cultural life and the spiritual and cultural diversification of humanity.

In this general perspective the Jewish people has a part to play as an example of cultural and spiritual persistence in the face of continuous physical discouragement. It has shown a unique aptitude for transcending the law that man is what he does. Its physical life—its means of making a livelihood—was dictated for nearly two thousands years by the outside world, or by many outside worlds; its spiritual and cultural life was conditioned by an inner world. This has been so singular a phenomenon that one can understand the incredulity of those who declare that no such inner world exists, that there is only a shell with nothing inside; that is, there is no Jewish peoplehood, only a simulacrum. To hold such a view one must be ignorant of the inner Jewish world. Others, better informed, go to the opposite extreme; they are so impressed by the performance that they ask the Jewish people to keep it up forever without the reinforcement of a Jewish homeland. How much more impressive that would be as an example! But though better informed, they fail to see that the cohesive force of the Jewish tradition was the hope of seeing the Jewish homeland reconstituted. That the hope was a vital, interpenetrating thing is proved by its power to hold the Jews together throughout the centuries of the Exile. It is proved even more strikingly by the event: the moment they stopped believing that a Messiah would rebuild their homeland, they set about building it themselves, and the reality holds them together even as the hope did.

The great question is: Will the power of the reality be as durable as the power of the hope? The world role of the Jewish people was woven into the Messianic hope of the Return. The Return itself was seen as signalizing the beginning of a new world order. Now the reality of the Return is before us, incomplete and imperfect, and it does carry with it the suggestion of a new world order, for it became a reality through the first fumbling attempts to institute a world organization of peoples, the League of Nations and the United Nations. If it loses the sense of a world role in an egotistical narrowing down and emasculating of the reality, if it becomes provincial, the Jewish people will simply disappear; it will have done with a tremendous effort what it could have done with no effort at all.

The hope, as long as it was a hope, inspired the Jewish people to demonstrate the primacy of the spirit over the material. Amid displacements, in exile, poverty, and persecution, it found the source of life in the mind. If it can continue to do so with the Exile approaching an end, with displacement, poverty, and persecution diminished for the greatest part of it, if it can continue as one people, a world people with a world function, it will fulfill the Zionist purpose. It will take its place among those forces that are struggling to liberate man from enslavement to physical circumstances. It will participate as one of the leaders in the double process that contains man's only hope: the universal conquest of want by technology, the universal enrichment of life by the acceptance and encouragement of culture-creating units.

The greatest obstacle to the realization of this vision is the weariness and disenchantment that regard it only as a vision. It is perhaps the particular usefulness of the Jewish people that, with much more occasion than any other, it has not become weary and disenchanted.

A Note About the Author

Born in Rumania in 1895, Maurice Samuel was educated in England, and came to the United States in 1914. After serving in the U.S. Army in France, he became an interpreter at the Peace Conference and with the Reparations Commissions in Berlin and Vienna, returning to America in 1921. Since then he has traveled extensively throughout the United States, Western Europe, Africa, and the Near East, partly as lecturer and partly to acquire information. His major interest for nearly fifty years has been the position of the Jewish people in the Western world; of his twenty books, fifteen are concerned with the exposition of Jewish values or examine the relations between the Jewish and Christian worlds. Mr. Samuel is married and lives in New York City.

A Note on the Type

The text of this book has been set on the Linotype in a type face called "Baskerville." The face is a facsimile reproduction of type cast from molds made for JOHN BASKERVILLE (1706–1775) from his designs. The punches for the revived Linotype Baskerville were cut under the supervision of the English printer George W. Jones.

John Baskerville's original face was one of the forerunners of the type style known as "modern face" to printers: a "modern" of the period A.D. 1800.

Composed, printed, and bound by
The Haddon Craftsmen, Inc., Scranton, Pa.